Biological Warfare

Other Books of Related Interest:

Opposing Viewpoints Series

Bioterrorism

At Issue Series

Biological and Chemical Weapons

Current Controversies Series

Resistant Infections

"Congress shall make
no law . . . abridging
the freedom of speech,
or of the press."

First Amendment to the U.S. Constitution

The basic foundation of our democracy is the First Amendment guarantee of freedom of expression. The Opposing Viewpoints Series is dedicated to the concept of this basic freedom and the idea that it is more important to practice it than to enshrine it.

OPPOSING VIEWPOINTS® SERIES

Biological Warfare

Christine Watkins, book editor

GREENHAVEN PRESS
A part of Gale, Cengage Learning

GALE
CENGAGE Learning™

Detroit • New York • San Francisco • New Haven, Conn • Waterville, Maine • London

GALE
CENGAGE Learning™

Christine Nasso, *Publisher*
Elizabeth Des Chenes, *Managing Editor*

© 2010 Greenhaven Press, a part of Gale, Cengage Learning.

Gale and Greenhaven Press are registered trademarks used herein under license.

For more information, contact:
Greenhaven Press
27500 Drake Rd.
Farmington Hills, MI 48331-3535
Or you can visit our Internet site at gale.cengage.com

Articles in Greenhaven Press anthologies are often edited for length to meet page requirements. In addition, original titles of these works are changed to clearly present the main thesis and to explicitly indicate the author's opinion. Every effort is made to ensure that Greenhaven Press accurately reflects the original intent of the authors. Every effort has been made to trace the owners of copyrighted material.

Cover Image copyright © Moori/Dreamstime.com.

LIBRARY OF CONGRESS CATALOGING-IN-PUBLICATION DATA

Biological warfare / Christine Watkins, book editor.
    p. cm. -- (Opposing viewpoints)
    Includes bibliographical references and index.
    ISBN 978-0-7377-4757-7 (hardcover) -- ISBN 978-0-7377-4758-4 (pbk.)
    1. Biological warfare--Juvenile literature. I. Watkins, Christine, 1951-
    UG447.8.B5643 2010
    358'.38--dc22   2009045721

Printed in the United States of America
1 2 3 4 5 6 7 14 13 12 11 10

Contents

Chapter 3: How Should the United States Prepare for Biological Warfare?

Chapter 4: How Can Biological Warfare Be Prevented?

Why Consider Opposing Viewpoints?

> "The only way in which a human being can make some approach to knowing the whole of a subject is by hearing what can be said about it by persons of every variety of opinion and studying all modes in which it can be looked at by every character of mind. No wise man ever acquired his wisdom in any mode but this."
>
> John Stuart Mill

In our media-intensive culture it is not difficult to find differing opinions. Thousands of newspapers and magazines and dozens of radio and television talk shows resound with differing points of view. The difficulty lies in deciding which opinion to agree with and which "experts" seem the most credible. The more inundated we become with differing opinions and claims, the more essential it is to hone critical reading and thinking skills to evaluate these ideas. Opposing Viewpoints books address this problem directly by presenting stimulating debates that can be used to enhance and teach these skills. The varied opinions contained in each book examine many different aspects of a single issue. While examining these conveniently edited opposing views, readers can develop critical thinking skills such as the ability to compare and contrast authors' credibility, facts, argumentation styles, use of persuasive techniques, and other stylistic tools. In short, the Opposing Viewpoints Series is an ideal way to attain the higher-level thinking and reading skills so essential in a culture of diverse and contradictory opinions.

In addition to providing a tool for critical thinking, Opposing Viewpoints books challenge readers to question their own strongly held opinions and assumptions. Most people form their opinions on the basis of upbringing, peer pressure, and personal, cultural, or professional bias. By reading carefully balanced opposing views, readers must directly confront new ideas as well as the opinions of those with whom they disagree. This is not to simplistically argue that everyone who reads opposing views will—or should—change his or her opinion. Instead, the series enhances readers' understanding of their own views by encouraging confrontation with opposing ideas. Careful examination of others' views can lead to the readers' understanding of the logical inconsistencies in their own opinions, perspective on why they hold an opinion, and the consideration of the possibility that their opinion requires further evaluation.

Evaluating Other Opinions

To ensure that this type of examination occurs, Opposing Viewpoints books present all types of opinions. Prominent spokespeople on different sides of each issue as well as well-known professionals from many disciplines challenge the reader. An additional goal of the series is to provide a forum for other, less known, or even unpopular viewpoints. The opinion of an ordinary person who has had to make the decision to cut off life support from a terminally ill relative, for example, may be just as valuable and provide just as much insight as a medical ethicist's professional opinion. The editors have two additional purposes in including these less known views. One, the editors encourage readers to respect others' opinions—even when not enhanced by professional credibility. It is only by reading or listening to and objectively evaluating others' ideas that one can determine whether they are worthy of consideration. Two, the inclusion of such viewpoints encourages the important critical thinking skill of objectively evaluating an author's credentials and bias. This evaluation will illuminate an author's reasons for taking a particular stance on an issue and will aid in readers' evaluation of the author's ideas.

It is our hope that these books will give readers a deeper understanding of the issues debated and an appreciation of the complexity of even seemingly simple issues when good and honest people disagree. This awareness is particularly important in a democratic society such as ours in which people enter into public debate to determine the common good. Those with whom one disagrees should not be regarded as enemies but rather as people whose views deserve careful examination and may shed light on one's own.

Thomas Jefferson once said that "difference of opinion leads to inquiry, and inquiry to truth." Jefferson, a broadly educated man, argued that "if a nation expects to be ignorant and free . . . it expects what never was and never will be." As individuals and as a nation, it is imperative that we consider the opinions of others and examine them with skill and discernment. The Opposing Viewpoints Series is intended to help readers achieve this goal.

David L. Bender and Bruno Leone,
Founders

Introduction

"Thanks to biotechnology, researchers worldwide are developing new vaccines to combat both long-standing and newly emerging viruses. . . . When used negligently, or misused deliberately, biotechnology could inflict the most profound human suffering—ranging from the accidental release of disease agents into the environment to intentional disease outbreaks caused by state or non-state actors."

Kofi Annan, former
United Nations secretary-general,
November 18, 2006

Biological warfare is the deliberate use of pathogens— bacteria, viruses, or other disease-causing microbes—for the purpose of incapacitating or killing humans, livestock, or crops. Although it has gained attention in recent years, biological warfare dates back to the beginning of recorded history. As examples, in the sixth century B.C., the Assyrians were purported to have poisoned the wells of their enemies with fungus; during the Middle Ages, bubonic plague–infested animals and diseased human corpses were used to sicken opposing armies; and in the eighteenth century, Indian tribes poisoned the British by spiking their water sources with bacteria. The United States began its own offensive biological warfare program in 1943, and by 1969 had weaponized several biological agents including anthrax, botulism, and Venezuelan equine encephalitis. These were all destroyed, however, after President Richard Nixon ended the program in 1969. And with hopes of ridding the world of all biological warfare, twenty-two state parties—the United States included—signed the 1972 Biological Weapons Convention (BWC, which became effective March 26, 1975), stating that they would never develop, produce, stockpile, acquire, or retain biological warfare agents or the means to deliver them. As of July 2008, 162 nation-states are signatories of the Biological Weapons Convention. Certain nations—Egypt, Iran, Israel, Syria, North Korea, China, and Russia among them—are suspected of continued involvement with biological weapons programs. Because of a category of scientific research referred to as "dual-use" biotechnology, however, such concerns about the proliferation of bioweapons are difficult to verify or disprove.

The dual-use dilemma comes during a time of extraordinary technological advances in science and medicine that have led to the development of new drugs and medical breakthroughs with which to fight the global spread of infectious diseases. The dilemma arises because the same research used to prevent disease can also be used to create disease. "At the same time that [biotechnology] has benefitted humanity by enabling advances in medicine and agriculture, it has also increased the availability of pathogens and technologies that can be used for sinister purposes," stated the U.S. Commission on the Prevention of Weapons of Mass Destruction Proliferation and Terrorism in a December 2008 report titled *Biotechnology Research in an Age of Terrorism*, which is often referred to as the Fink Report after the committee chairman, Dr. Gerald Fink. Among other areas of concern, the report singled out specific experiments that are being undertaken to (1) enhance the virulence of a pathogen, (2) increase transmissibility of a pathogen, and (3) enable weaponization of a biological agent. Many members of the American public believe that these research laboratories do not have sufficient oversight and accountability to ensure safety and security and are thereby putting the nation in danger of a possible accidental pathogen release, or a deliberate terrorist attack should the biotechnology fall into the wrong hands. As Judy Winters wrote in her April 2008 article "The National Bio Agro Defense Facility's 'Dual Use' Research, a Threat to Our Nation's Security," for *OpEd News*, "Biotechnology in the hands of a rogue government, a terrorist, or a simple act of greed and someone's willingness to sell a product or an associated technology on the black market would have the unprecedented potential for destructive and deadly widespread applications as a bioweapon."

Thus, one of the most difficult and pressing issues that the United States and the international community must resolve is how to manage the risk associated with the misuse of technology for biological warfare purposes, yet still allow the growth of critical research for the health and benefit of humanity. The authors in *Opposing Viewpoints: Biological Warfare* discuss this issue and many others regarding the threat of biological warfare in the following chapters: "How Great a Danger Do Biological Weapons Pose?" "Who Constitutes a Serious Biological Warfare Threat?" "How Should the United States Prepare for Biological Warfare?" and "How Can Biological Warfare Be Prevented?"

OPPOSING
VIEWPOINTS®
SERIES

CHAPTER 1

How Great a Danger Do Biological Weapons Pose?

Chapter Preface

In 2003 a Michigan supermarket employee intentionally contaminated two hundred pounds of ground beef with pesticide, which sickened ninety-two people. In 2007 pet food laced with the chemical melamine sickened many cats and dogs, and in some cases led to the animals' deaths, prompting the recall of hundreds of pet food products. Melamine turned up in China the following year in baby formula, which caused thousands of children to become ill, some of whom died. Spinach tainted with E. coli, peanuts contaminated with salmonella—all of these incidents have heightened awareness among Americans that the nation's food supply can be a potential target for terrorists. As former secretary of health and human services Tommy Thompson said in 2004, "I, for the life of me, cannot understand why terrorists have not attacked our food supply, because it is so easy to do."

The Food and Drug Administration (FDA) is the federal agency responsible for overseeing the safety of most food (including animal feed) in the United States, with the exception of meat, poultry, and processed egg products, which are regulated by the United States Department of Agriculture (USDA). The FDA, however, is considered to be understaffed and underfunded, and many health advocates believe it does not exert sufficient control over the quality and content of imported food. Much of the problem lies in the fact that food-safety systems were developed when most of the nation's food was grown and prepared locally, but the increasing globalization of the food chain and the rising volume of imports have created enormous challenges with respect to the safe manufacturing and processing of food. "The United States is particularly dependent on foreign nations for foodstuffs," said Steven Nissen, Cleveland Clinic cardiologist who advocates for FDA reform. "Eighty percent of seafood and nearly half of the fresh fruits consumed in this country come from abroad. Much of it clears customs based on electronic data provided by the importer, without any U.S. sampling or testing." For its part, the FDA has addressed these challenges by collaborating with representatives from many foreign countries to expand the FDA's presence and capacity for the regulation of food. "FDA has also made a commitment to station agency representatives in China to increase our ability to carry out foreign inspections and to assist the Chinese government officials in their regulatory work associated with FDA-regulated products that are to be exported to the United States," former FDA associate commissioner for foods David Acheson told the U.S. House of Representatives Subcommittee on Oversight and Investigations in 2008. The FDA also hopes to establish foreign offices in India, Europe, the Middle East, and Central and South America.

Bioterrorism through the food supply is a frightening concept, but skeptics believe such an assault would prove too difficult to execute successfully. To be an effective killer, a pathogen must be very deadly with a long incubation period and difficult to detect; most contaminants often change the taste, odor, and consistency of food, making them easily detectible. In addition, the virulent strain would need to be manufactured in sufficient quantities to be effective and then shipped to the place of distribution. As Fred Burton and Scott Stewart wrote in their article "Placing the Terrorist Threat to the Food Supply in Perspective" for *Right Side News*, "From a cost benefit standpoint, it would be much cheaper and easier to use explosives to create disruption than it would be to execute a complicated plot against the food supply."

Experts debate the possibility of a bioterrorist attack against the United States' food supply. Both sides, however, agree on one point: Even if such an attack by a terrorist group such as al Qaeda, a smaller extremist organization, or a single individual had only limited success, it could still cause enough panic and disruption to result in significant economic hardship. The authors in this chapter discuss additional issues concerning the risks associated with the use of biological warfare against the United States.

| "A number of terrorist organizations and rogue individuals have sought to acquire and use biological or toxin agents."

Biological Weapons Pose a Serious Threat to Americans

Commission on the Prevention of WMD Proliferation and Terrorism and Senator Bob Graham

Led by senators Bob Graham and Jim Talent, the Commission on the Prevention of Weapons of Mass Destruction (WMD) Proliferation and Terrorism was developed to assess the nation's activities, initiatives, and programs to prevent the proliferation of weapons of mass destruction. In the following viewpoint, the commission contends that several countries and terrorist organizations have biological weapons programs already in place or are actively seeking to acquire deadly pathogens to use for biological warfare. Additionally, scientists are developing biotechnology that could lead to the creation of newer and deadlier biological weapons.

Commission on the Prevention of WMD Proliferation and Terrorism and Senator Bob Graham, *World at Risk: The Report of the Commission on the Prevention of WMD Proliferation and Terrorism.* New York: Vintage Books, 2008. Reproduced by permission of The Citizens Foundation USA.

As you read, consider the following questions:

1. According to the Commission on the Prevention of WMD Proliferation and Terrorism, why is the anthrax bacterium considered an ideal biological warfare agent?

2. As explained in the viewpoint, is anthrax highly contagious?

3. In what respect is the biological weapons threat greater than the nuclear weapons threat, according to the commission?

Biological weapons are disease-causing microbes (chiefly bacteria and viruses) and toxins (poisonous substances produced by living creatures) that have been harnessed for the purpose of incapacitating or killing humans, livestock, or crops. Examples include the bacteria that cause anthrax and plague, the viruses that cause smallpox and Ebola hemorrhagic fever, and poisons of natural origin such as ricin and botulinum toxin.

Each of these agents has distinct characteristics that affect its suitability for use as a weapon. These are *infectivity* (the ability to infect a human host and cause disease), *virulence* (the severity of the resulting illness), *transmissibility* (the ability of the disease to spread from person to person), and *persistence* (the duration of a microbe's survival after its release into the environment).

The process of turning a natural pathogen into a WMD [weapon of mass destruction] begins with acquiring a sample of a disease-causing microbe from a natural source (such as a person or sick animal) or stealing it from a laboratory or culture collection. But just as a bullet is a harmless lump of lead without a cartridge and a rifle to deliver it, most pathogens and toxins are not effective weapons in their natural state and must be processed ("weaponized") and combined with a delivery system to make them capable of producing large numbers of casualties.

The Anthrax Threat

The anthrax bacterium is considered an ideal biological warfare agent because it is relatively easy to grow, highly lethal when inhaled, and able to transform itself into a hearty spore that can persist in soil or contaminate a target area for years. If an individual is treated with antibiotics shortly after inhaling anthrax spores, the infection can usually be cured. If treatment is delayed, however, the bacterial toxins will be released, and extraordinary medical intervention is then needed for the victim to have any chance of survival.

Despite the small quantity of dried anthrax spores used in the [United States] 2001 letter attacks—a total of about 15 grams—the ripple effects of the mailings extended far beyond those sickened or killed. Professor Leonard Cole of Rutgers University has estimated the total economic impact of the anthrax letter attacks at more than $6 billion. If only 15 grams of dry anthrax spores delivered by mail could produce such an enormous effect, the consequences of a large-scale aerosol release would be almost unimaginable.

As deadly as anthrax can be, it fortunately is not contagious. Because persons infected with the disease cannot transmit it to others, only those who are directly exposed to anthrax spores are at risk. Contagious diseases such as plague or smallpox, in contrast, can be transmitted through person-to-person contact, turning the initial set of victims into secondary sources of infection.

Many factors would affect the outcome of a biological attack, including the type and strain of agent; the time of day that it is released, and the prevailing wind, weather, and atmospheric conditions; and the basic health of the people who are exposed to it. Also important are the speed and manner in which public health authorities and medical professionals detect and respond to the resulting outbreak. A prompt response with effective medical countermeasures such as antibiotics and vaccination can potentially blunt the impact of an attack and thwart the terrorists' objectives.

The State Threat

During the Cold War, both the United States and the Soviet Union produced and stockpiled biological agents. But in November 1969, the [Richard M.] Nixon administration renounced the U.S. offensive biological weapons program and then began to destroy its stockpile. This unilateral action opened the way to the successful negotiation of the 1972 Biological Weapons Convention (BWC), a multilateral treaty banning the development, production, and stockpiling of biological and toxin weapons.

Although the BWC was supposed to end all efforts by states to develop the capability to employ disease as a weapon, it has unfortunately failed to achieve this goal. Because the materials and equipment needed to produce biowarfare agents also have legitimate uses in scientific research and commercial industry, it is difficult to verify the BWC with any degree of confidence. A number of countries have secretly violated the treaty. The most egregious case was that of the Soviet Union, which created a massive biological weapons development and production complex employing more than 50,000 scientists and technicians.

Today, several important countries—Egypt, Israel, and Syria among them—remain outside the Biological Weapons Convention. The U.S. State Department has also expressed concern that some parties to the treaty such as Russia, China, North Korea, and Iran may be pursuing offensive biological weapons programs in secret.

The Non-State Threat

States do not have a monopoly on biological weapons. In the past, a number of terrorist organizations and rogue individuals have sought to acquire and use biological or toxin agents. Such weapons may be attractive to terrorists because of their potential to inflict mass casualties or to be used covertly. In addition, as the anthrax letter attacks of autumn 2001 clearly demonstrated, even small-scale attacks of limited lethality can elicit a disproportionate amount of terror and social disruption.

The 2001 anthrax mailings were not the first incident of bioterrorism in the United States. In 1984, the Rajneeshees, a religious cult in Oregon, sought to reduce voter turnout and win control of the county government in an upcoming election by temporarily incapacitating local residents with a bacterial infection. In a test run of this scheme in September 1984, cult members contaminated 10 restaurant salad bars in a town in Oregon with salmonella, a common bacterium that causes food poisoning. The attack sickened 751 people, some seriously.

A decade later, members of a Japanese doomsday cult called Aum Shinrikyo released anthrax bacterial spores from the roof of a building in Tokyo. Fortunately, this attack failed because the cult produced and dispersed a harmless strain of anthrax that is used as a veterinary vaccine. Had Aum succeeded in acquiring a virulent strain and delivered it effectively, the casualties could have been in the thousands.

Islamist terrorist groups such as al Qaeda have also sought to acquire biological weapons in the past. Former CIA [Central Intelligence Agency] director George Tenet wrote in his memoir that in 1999, in parallel with planning for the September 11 [2001] terrorist attacks, al Qaeda launched a concerted effort to develop an anthrax weapon that could inflict mass casualties. The group hired a Pakistani veterinarian named Rauf Ahmad to set up a bioweapons laboratory in Afghanistan, but he became disgruntled with the amount of money he was paid and eventually quit. To continue the anthrax work, al Qaeda then hired a Malaysian terrorist, Yazid Sufaat, who had studied biology at California State University in Sacramento. But in December 2001, after the U.S. invasion of Afghanistan, Sufaat fled; he was captured by authorities as he tried to sneak back into Malaysia.

The cases of the Rajneeshees, Aum Shinrikyo, and al Qaeda underscore not only the dangerous potential of bioterrorism but also the technical difficulties that terrorist groups seeking such weapons are likely to encounter. Aum's failure to carry out a mass-casualty attack, despite its access to scientific expertise and ample financial resources, suggests that one should not oversimplify or exaggerate the threat of bioterrorism. Developing a biological weapon that can inflict mass casualties is an intricate undertaking, both technically and operationally complex.

The Threat from Biologists

Because of the difficulty of weaponizing and disseminating significant quantities of a biological agent in aerosol form, government officials and outside experts believe that no terrorist group currently has an operational capability to carry out a mass-casualty attack. But they could develop that capability quickly. In 2006 congressional testimony, Charles E. Allen, under secretary for intelligence and analysis at the Department of Homeland Security, noted that the threat of bioterrorism could increase rapidly if a terrorist group were able to recruit technical experts who had experience in a national biological warfare program, with knowledge comparable to that of the perpetrator of the 2001 anthrax letter attacks. In other words, given the high level of know-how needed to use disease as a weapon to cause mass casualties, the United States should be less concerned that terrorists will become biologists and far more concerned that biologists will become terrorists.

Biological Threat Risk Assessment

The threat posed by biological agents employed in a terrorist attack on the United States is arguably the most important homeland security challenge of our era. Whether natural pathogens are cultured or new variants are bioengineered, the consequence of a terrorist-induced pandemic could be millions of casualties—far more than we would expect from nuclear terrorism, chemical attacks, or conventional attacks on the infrastructure of the United States such as the attacks of September 11, 2001. Even if there were fewer casualties, additional second-order consequences (including psychological, social, and economic effects) would dramatically compound the effects. Bioengineering is no longer the exclusive purview of state sponsors of terrorism; this technology is now available to small terrorist groups and even to deranged individuals.

Gregory S. Parnell, Luciana L. Borio,
Gerald G. Brown, David Banks, and Alyson G. Wilson,
"Scientists Urge DHS to Improve Bioterrorism Risk Assessment,"
Biosecurity and Bioterrorism, *vol. 6, no. 4, 2008.*

The last point bears repeating. We accept the validity of intelligence estimates about the current rudimentary nature of terrorist capabilities in the area of biological weapons but caution that the terrorists are trying to upgrade their capabilities and could do so by recruiting skilled scientists. In this respect the biological threat is greater than the nuclear; the acquisition of deadly pathogens, and their weaponization and dissemination in aerosol form, would entail fewer technical hurdles than the theft or production of weapons-grade uranium or plutonium and its assembly into an improvised nuclear device.

The difficulty of quantifying the bioterrorism threat to the United States does not make that threat any less real or compelling. It involves both motivation and capability, and the first ingredient is clearly present. Al Qaeda had an active biological weapons program in the past, and it is unlikely that the group has lost interest in employing infectious disease as a weapon. That roughly a half-dozen countries are suspected to possess or to be seeking biological weapons also provides ample grounds for concern.

The Future Threat

In addition to the current threat of bioweapons proliferation and terrorism, a set of over-the-horizon risks is emerging, associated with recent advances in the life sciences and biotechnology and the worldwide diffusion of these capabilities. Over the past few decades, scientists have gained a deep understanding of the structure of genetic material (DNA) and its role in directing the operation of living cells. This knowledge has led to remarkable gains in the treatment of disease and holds the promise of future medical breakthroughs. The industrial applications of this knowledge are also breathtaking: It is now possible to engineer microorganisms to give them new and beneficial characteristics.

Activity has been particularly intense in the area of biotechnology known as *synthetic genomics*. Since the early 1980s, scientists have developed automated machines that can synthesize long strands of DNA coding for genes and even entire microbial genomes. By piecing together large fragments of genetic material synthesized in the laboratory, scientists have been able to assemble infectious viruses, including the polio virus and the formerly extinct 1918 strain of the influenza virus, which was responsible for the global pandemic that killed between 20 million and 40 million people.

As DNA synthesis technology continues to advance at a rapid pace, it will soon become feasible to synthesize nearly any virus whose DNA sequence has been decoded—such as the smallpox virus, which was eradicated from nature in 1977—as well as artificial microbes that do not exist in nature. This growing ability to engineer life at the molecular level carries with it the risk of facilitating the development of new and more deadly biological weapons.

The only way to rule out the harmful use of advances in biotechnology would be to stifle their beneficial applications as well—and that is not a realistic option. Instead, the dual-use dilemma associated with the revolution in biology must be managed on an ongoing basis. As long as rapid innovations in biological science and the malevolent intentions of terrorists and proliferators continue on trajectories that are likely to intersect sooner or later, the risk that biological weapons pose to humanity must not be minimized or ignored.

| "At this time, there is simply not enough data to suggest that biological weapons should occupy the same policy category as nuclear weapons."

Biological Weapons Are Less Destructive than Nuclear Weapons

Allison Macfarlane

In the following viewpoint, Allison Macfarlane explains that most people consider weapons of mass destruction to include biological, chemical, and nuclear weapons. Macfarlane contends, however, that nuclear weapons are far more destructive than biological or chemical weapons—in human life toll and infrastructure—and should not be considered equal to them with regard to national defense policy and spending. Macfarlane is an associate professor at the Massachusetts Institute of Technology. Her research focuses on international security and environmental policy issues associated with nuclear weapons and nuclear energy.

Allison Macfarlane, *Audit of the Conventional Wisdom: All Weapons of Mass Destruction Are Not Equal.* Fairfax, VA: Center for International Studies, Massachusetts Institute of Technology, 2005. Reproduced by permission of the publisher and the author.

As you read, consider the following questions:

1. In the author's opinion, why is it difficult to determine the lethal capability of biological weapons?

2. Have there been substantiated new instances of biological weapons proliferation, according to Allison Macfarlane?

3. Has the United States implied that it would retaliate using nuclear weapons if attacked with chemical or biological weapons, according to the author?

There is some truth to the U.S. concern about weapons of mass destruction (WMD). The September 11, 2001 attacks showed that terrorists have become intent on causing as much death and destruction as possible. There are numerous reports that al Qaeda has sought to acquire WMD. Terrorists are not the only ones interested in such weapons: Currently there are eight states with nuclear weapons, sixteen with chemical weapons programs, and five to twelve with biological weapons programs.

Partly in response, the United States has based recent nuclear weapons targeting policy on the concept of a broadly conceived WMD threat, equating nuclear weapons with biological and chemical ones. Moreover, the United States is still involved in a war in Iraq that it waged in large part because of the WMD threat. The United States spends $7 billion on biodefense but less than $2 billion preventing a nuclear attack [as of 2005]. These developments beg the question: Are biological and chemical weapons really as threatening to the United States as nuclear weapons?

Defining Weapons of Mass Destruction

The first step in trying to answer this question is to determine how the concept of weapons of mass destruction is used, what these weapons can actually do, and whether we can protect ourselves against them. Then it will be clearer whether these weapons really occupy the same category. The new perspective we gain on the concept of weapons of mass destruction will help us grasp the implications for foreign and domestic policies.

The term weapons of mass destruction was first used on December 28, 1937, in a London *Times* article on the aerial bombing of Spanish cities by the Germans, noting, "Who can think without horror of what another widespread war would mean, waged as it would be with all the new weapons of mass destruction?" The United Nations has used this term since 1947, defining it as "atomic explosive weapons, radioactive material weapons, lethal chemical and biological weapons, and any weapons developed in the future which have characteristics comparable in destructive effect to those of the atomic bomb or other weapons mentioned above." The [George W.] Bush administration defines WMD as nuclear, chemical, and biological weapons, currently the most common understanding of the term.

WMD use must involve mass casualties, especially deaths. In some situations, conventional weapons have created "mass destruction," such as the fire bombings by allied troops during the Second World War. Civilians were targeted, and the deaths numbered in the tens of thousands for Dresden [Germany] and 100,000 for Tokyo [Japan]. A true WMD would create similar casualties with a single weapon.

Understanding the Capabilities of Weapons of Mass Destruction

Nuclear weapons destroy not only human lives but also infrastructure. We know from the atomic bombs dropped on Hiroshima and Nagasaki the destructive power of these weapons. In Hiroshima, the 15-kiloton bomb killed 140,000 people; in Nagasaki, the 21-kiloton device killed 70,000. Both of these cities were turned into wastelands from the blasts' shock waves and associated fires. Modern nuclear weapons in the stockpiles of nuclear weapons states (of which there are about 30,000) average more than 100 kilotons yield.

A chemical weapon attack on a city could be expected to produce a maximum of thousands of deaths. During the First World War, "successful" gas attacks would use tons of gas and produce hundreds to thousands of deaths and thousands of injured. An Office of Technology Assessment report suggests 1,000 kilograms of sarin gas aerially dispersed on a city of density 3,000 to 10,000 people per square kilometer would result in 300 to 8,000 deaths, depending on the climatic conditions at the time of the attack. The "success" of a chemical weapons attack depends on the purity of the agent; climatic factors, such as wind, cloud cover, temperature, and precipitation; the physical properties of the chemical, including density, vapor pressure, and boiling point; persistence in the environment; and delivery mechanism. Moreover, the lethality of a chemical weapons attack depends on whether the targets are defended. Gas masks and protective clothing provide full protection against chemical weapons—defenses that do not exist for explosive or incendiary attack.

Biological weapons are more difficult to characterize in terms of lethality. The reason for this is perhaps a good one: A large-scale biological weapons attack using well-dispersed agent has never occurred. The Office of Technology Assessment estimated that depending on climate conditions, 100kg of anthrax could result in 130,000 to 3,000,000 dead in an urban region of 3,000 to 10,000 people per square kilometer.

Actually, a number of studies of biological weapons' lethality generate an enormous range, from 66 deaths to 88 billion deaths per kilogram of agent used for anthrax. This variance underscores the uncertainty involved in predicting the lethality of these agents as weapons. A National Academy of Sciences report pointed out that "modeling efforts over the past decade, at least those publicly available, tend to emphasize worst-case scenarios—broadscale attacks involving millions of human casualties, if not fatalities."

Defending Against Weapons of Mass Destruction

The ability of a target population to defend itself against the use of nuclear, chemical, or biological weapons varies widely. Against nuclear weapons there is very limited defense possible. The national missile defense program—designed to intercept incoming warheads—may never be able to solve the problem posed by countermeasures, warheads loaded with hundreds of thousands of bomblets containing biological agent or decoys that fool the interceptor. It cannot defend against a nuclear bomb delivered surreptitiously, such as by cargo container ship. Defense against nuclear attack, then, takes the form of preventing the spread of nuclear weapons, materials, and expertise, a more difficult task. In contrast, it is possible to mount defenses against chemical and biological weapons. Detection of attack, use of protective clothing, and administration of antidotes, vaccines, and other treatment can greatly reduce casualties. . . .

Some experts consider biological and nuclear weapons to be the "true" weapons of mass destruction. The higher end of the lethality range of biological weapons is certainly in the realm of the threat posed by nuclear weapons, but the range itself is troubling. If a nuclear weapon goes off in a densely populated area, it will kill tens of thousands of people. It is not possible to make the same assertion for biological weapons. The extremely uncertain estimates of deaths from bioweapons rely on simulations that use limited data sets. For instance, one significant source of uncertainty is the lethality of the agent such as anthrax and modified (genetically or antibiotic-resistant) agents. These simulations describe worst-case scenarios and do not consider the ameliorating effects of defenses such as a good public health system. A bioweapon attack on the heart of a poor, overcrowded, third-world city may indeed result in the high death rates suggested in some models. But is the United States as vulnerable? Hardly. It has an extensive public health system and has invested in biological weapons defenses. At this time, there is simply not enough data to suggest that biological weapons should occupy the same policy category as nuclear weapons.

Instilling Fear About Weapons of Mass Destruction

What are the political and economic implications of equating biological and chemical weapons with nuclear ones? Americans are living in a state of fear of attack by WMD. The United States is now targeting non-nuclear weapons states with nuclear weapons and in the process is increasing the value of nuclear, chemical, and biological weapons. Moreover, the United States is spending far more money on biodefense measures than for nuclear defense.

News reports and politicians try to convince the public of the threat posed by WMD. Consider this statement from President [George W.] Bush: "Those attacks [of September, 11, 2001] also raised the prospect of even worse dangers, of terrorists armed with chemical, biological, radiological and nuclear weapons. The possibility of secret and sudden attack with weapons of mass destruction is the greatest threat before humanity today." This kind of rhetoric leads the public to believe that an attack is imminent and would be equally destructive, no matter which weapon is used. Statements like this suggest that proliferation of these weapons is on the rise.

The only actual proliferation that has taken place over the last few years is nuclear weapons proliferation by North Korea, Libya (now disarmed), and perhaps Iran. There are no known new instances of biological or chemical weapons proliferation by states. Moreover, warnings of bioweapons attack are out of proportion to the threat. (And indeed few people die each year from terrorist attacks—even during 2001, when 2,988 died in the 9/11 attacks; that same year in the United States, 3,923 died by drowning.) Though a bioweapons attack might be expected to kill up to thousands, it most likely wouldn't reach the number of traffic deaths per year (40,000-odd).

The fear of bioweapons attack is in itself a problem. The dire warnings communicated by the U.S. government and the media could lead to panic and chaos, resulting in more deaths than if a calmer and more rational approach were used. Instead, Americans could be told that in the event of a bioweapons attack they should take precautions similar to those that prevent the transmission of any infectious disease (washing hands frequently, etc.). By doing so, fewer would likely die. More resources to strengthen the public health system would also boost confidence, trust, and protection.

Responding with a Nuclear Threat

One of the main U.S. foreign policy tools that relies heavily on the concept of WMD is the 2002 *Nuclear Posture Review.* In establishing the size of the nuclear force for the United States, it claims

> the emergence of a new, hostile military coalition against the United States or its allies in which one or more members possesses WMD and the means of delivery is a potential contingency that could have major consequences for U.S. defense planning, including plans for nuclear forces . . . North Korea, Iraq, Iran, Syria, and Libya are among the countries that could be involved in immediate, potential, or unexpected contingencies.

The 2002 *National Strategy to Combat Weapons of Mass Destruction* makes this policy more explicit, stating: "The United States will continue to make clear that it reserves the right to respond with overwhelming force—including through resort to all of our options—to the use of WMD against the

A Term of Mass Distraction

The term "Weapons of Mass Destruction" (WMD), used to encompass nuclear (NW), biological (BW), and chemical weapons (CW), is misleading, politically dangerous, and cannot be justified on grounds of military efficiency. . . . Whereas protection with various degrees of efficiency is possible against chemical and biological weapons, however inconvenient it might be for military forces on the battlefield and for civilians at home, it is not feasible at all against nuclear weapons. Chemical weapons have shown to be largely ineffective in warfare; biological weapons have never been deployed on any significant scale. Both types should be better designated as weapons of terror against civilians and weapons of intimidation for soldiers. Requirements on their transport system differ vastly from those for nuclear warheads. They are able to cause considerable anxiety, panic, and psychosis without borders within large parts of the population. Stockpiling of biological weapons is not possible over a long time scale. Only nuclear weapons are completely indiscriminate by their explosive power, heat radiation and radioactivity, and only they should therefore be called a weapon of mass destruction.

Gert G. Harigel,
"Chemical and Biological Weapons:
Use in Warfare, Impact on Society and Environment,"
Nuclear Age Peace Foundation, November 2001.

United States, our forces abroad, and friends and allies." The United States is suggesting that if attacked with chemical or biological weapons, it may respond with nuclear weapons.

In specifically identifying Iraq, Iran, Syria, and Libya, the United States reversed assurances it made in 1978 and 1995 that it would not attack non-nuclear weapons states with nuclear weapons. This new strategy has spawned more expansive policies such as that found in the classified appendix to a 2002 National Security Presidential Directive, which allows the use of preemptive attacks on nations or terrorists who are "close to acquiring" WMD and missiles that can transport them. The thinking goes like this: "The United States still needs nuclear weapons to deter a nuclear attack. But it must also . . . present a threat of nuclear retaliation to deter a biological attack, which could be as deadly, and which might not be deterred by the threat of U.S. conventional retaliation." But if biological weapons are not nearly as deadly as nuclear weapons, as I argue, then it follows that their use by states might very well be deterred by conventional weapons counterattack.

Instead of inhibiting attacks and proliferation of "weapons of mass destruction," these policies may encourage them. The U.S. WMD policies and biodefense programs inflate the capabilities of biological and chemical weapons. This exaggeration can translate to encouragement to states and terrorists to try to acquire these weapons. As suggested by the recent behavior of North Korea, Iraq, Iran, and Libya, nuclear weapons appear to be the most desirable weapons to states, but because of the ease of acquisition of biological and chemical weapons, these may be more desirable to non-state actors.

Spending for Weapons of Mass Destruction Defense

Equating nuclear weapons with biological weapons has important implications for U.S. domestic policy. Funds are being diverted to defend against and respond to future biological weapons attacks from more pressing issues. In a letter to *Science* magazine in 2005, more than 700 scientists expressed their concern about the massive redirection of funding from "projects of high public health importance to projects of high biodefense but low public health importance." Grants to work on bioweapons agents increased by 1,500 percent in the 2001–2005 period compared with 1996–2000. Similar increases in national biodefense spending exist. For FY[fiscal year]2001, the U.S. government spent $414 million on civilian biodefense; in FY2005, the budget request was $7,647.6 million, an increase of 1,850 percent.

A comparison of biodefense spending to nuclear security spending reveals the priorities of the U.S. government. As suggested earlier, the only defenses available against nuclear weapons attack are preventive: securing nuclear weapons, materials, and personnel around the world that could be used in a nuclear weapons program, and improving border security to detect the entry of a nuclear weapon into the United States. The United States has established a number of programs to this end. In FY2005, the U.S. government spent $803 million securing nuclear warheads, materials, and expertise in the former Soviet Union. The Department of Energy spent an additional $549 million in FY2005 to plan to dispose of U.S. weapons plutonium and uranium declared excess to military needs. In FY2006, the federal government requested $125 million for radiation portal monitors to protect the country's borders. Even when all these programs are considered together, the spending on defense against nuclear weapons use in the United States is less than $2 billion, much less than that spent on biodefense programs.

As the experience of the 1990s shows, nuclear weapons are the ones being proliferated. If they are the true weapons of mass destruction, then current U.S. policies do not make sense. Domestic defense against a biological weapons attack should not be receiving more than three times the funding as nuclear weapons defense strategies. Biological and chemical weapons are not nuclear weapons. In the event of a biological weapons attack, the U.S. may never determine who committed the attack, as it has not in the case of the 2001 anthrax attacks. [Editor's Note: In August 2008 the Department of Justice declared that it had identified the perpetrator of the anthrax attacks as Bruce E. Ivins, a governmental biodefense scientist.] Foreign policies that promise nuclear retaliation against those who attack with biological and chemical weapons are therefore weak threats. A stronger position to deal with the proliferation of these weapons would be to set policies that devalue nuclear, biological, and chemical weapons, instead of spending billions of dollars defending ourselves against ghosts, and in the process putting these weapons on a pedestal.

"We see the threat of an aerosolized anthrax attack as our number one bioterrorism concern, and it is that threat which we vigorously plan, invest, and intend to defeat."

Anthrax Is a Serious Threat

Jeffrey W. Runge

In the following viewpoint, Jeffrey W. Runge contends that al Qaeda is intent on developing biological weapons—possibly using anthrax—to attack the United States. Because such an attack would likely go undetected for several days, allowing the exposure to spread, the impact on a city's medical and emergency health sectors and its infrastructure could be catastrophic. Runge further advises that the United States use due diligence to develop and improve surveillance and response capabilities. Runge was the first chief medical officer for the U.S. Department of Homeland Security.

As you read, consider the following questions:

1. According to Jeffrey Runge, can a biological attack have long-term environmental effects?

Jeffrey W. Runge, "Testimony of Jeffrey W. Runge, MD Before the U.S. House of Representatives Committee on Homeland Security, Subcommittee on Emerging Threats, Cybersecurity, and Science and Technology," Department of Homeland Security, July 22, 2008. www.dhs.gov.

2. Is it likely that the United States will receive credible knowledge of an imminent biological attack before it occurs, in the author's opinion?

3. What is the BioWatch program, according to Runge?

Today I will discuss a number of important issues surrounding emerging biological threats and our nation's preparedness, including: the current biological threat environment as illustrated by the effect a biological attack might have in a city like Providence [Rhode Island], our approach to biosurveillance and environmental detection, and the roles and responsibilities of federal, state, [and] local [governments] and the private sector in response to and recovery from a biological attack. Providing this information to the public creates a more resilient public. By reducing the elements of surprise, fear, and panic, we can reduce the terror associated with such an event, making the public reaction a key part of the solution rather than the problem.

The Current Biological Threat

The risk of a large-scale biological attack on the nation is significant. We know that our terrorist enemies have sought to use biological agents as instruments of their warfare, and we believe that capability is within their reach.

I know many here today recall the anthrax attacks of 2001. As you know . . . certain buildings occupied by members of the legislative branch were temporarily closed while they were decontaminated. The magnitude of that terrorist attack is miniscule compared to the larger anthrax release envisioned by our enemies. It is nonetheless exemplary of the potential health and economic damage to which we are vulnerable. Unfortunately, the threat has not diminished since then—in fact, it has been building since well before the [terrorist] attacks of 9/11 [2001].

We know that in the late 1990s al Qaeda began developing a biological weapons program and constructed a low-tech facility in Qandahar [also spelled Kandahar], Afghanistan for anthrax production. Fortunately, U.S. military forces disrupted this activity and additional American and coalition operations in the region have damaged al Qaeda leadership and operational capabilities—but not their intent to use biological weapons. You will recall that in 2002, al Qaeda stated that they had the right to kill 4 million Americans—2 million of them children—and cripple thousands. An advisor to Bin Laden later issued a fatwa [religious opinion on Islamic law] on the permissibility of using weapons of mass destruction and increased the 4 million casualty figure to 10 million.

We have determined that al Qaeda seeks to develop and use a biological weapon to cause mass casualties in an attack on the homeland. Our analysis indicates that anthrax is a likely choice; and a successful single-city attack on an unprepared population could kill hundreds of thousands of citizens. A coordinated attack on multiple targets would come much closer in magnitude to our enemy's goal. Because of this, we see the threat of an aerosolized anthrax attack as our number one bioterrorism concern, and it is that threat which we vigorously plan, invest, and intend to defeat. Our efforts are not optional or discretionary. The ramifications of such an attack include tremendous loss of life, economic costs, damage to critical infrastructure, and unprecedented environmental contamination.

A biological attack would impact every sector of our society—not just the medical and public health communities. A biological attack respects no geographic or geopolitical boundary and will have an impact well beyond our nation's emergency departments and public health infrastructure. Absenteeism across multiple sectors due to illness, fear of contagion, or public health measures could threaten the function of critical infrastructure, the movement of goods and services, and the operation of our institutions. No federal department or agency will be exempt from the consequences of such an attack. Further, critical life-saving activities will depend on actions taken in the first few moments of the event. State and local governments will be called on to take several critical actions—alerting the public of the crisis without inciting panic; maintaining public confidence while making critical decisions; and bolstering local communities to rebound quickly.

As we work together to counter this threat, we must keep in mind that acts of biological terrorism don't go "bang." It could be hours or even days before we realize the full extent of an incident. Because of the lack of an explosion or immediate visual damage, many do not perceive the threat of bioterrorism to be as significant as that of a nuclear or conventional strike, even though such an attack could kill as many people as a nuclear detonation and have its own long-term environmental effects. This has caused a lack of public urgency in devoting significant resources to countering this threat—a luxury we simply cannot afford. . . .

Many people ask me, "What keeps you up at night?" It is the possibility of a large-scale biological attack on our homeland.

Threat Preparation Must Occur Nationwide

Given the challenges we face in assessing current terrorist capabilities and identifying plots, it is unlikely that we will receive actionable or specific warning of an imminent biological attack. Furthermore, many of these deadly biological agents, including anthrax, are readily available in nature, relatively easy to procure, culture, and weaponize. There are numerous domestic and international biological research programs using these agents for legitimate purposes, making it more difficult to separate the ill-intentioned research initiatives. As a result, it is unlikely that we will have credible knowledge of an imminent biological threat before it occurs.

This is why it is imperative that we continue to enhance our nation's efforts to disrupt biological plots, provide the earliest possible detection and warning of an attack, strengthen our preparedness and response efforts, and increase our capacity to quickly recover. . . .

While it is easy for us to assume that terrorists are only interested in striking major cities such as Washington, D.C., or New York City, we cannot ignore the attractiveness of softer targets to our enemies. On April 19, 1995, Oklahoma City experienced the horrors of terrorism when a truck bomb was detonated in front of the Alfred P. Murrah Federal Building, killing 168 people, including 19 children, and injuring hundreds more. Who would have thought that Oklahoma City would have been a target for terrorism? It is therefore imperative that all states and local jurisdictions are adequately prepared to handle events across the chemical, biological, radiological, and nuclear spectrum, as well as more conventional attacks or naturally occurring outbreaks.

The city of Providence, like many mid-sized cities, has a number of characteristics that make it potentially attractive as a target, such as its proximity to military assets, major metropolitan areas, and important transportation routes. An aerosolized sprayer releasing airborne anthrax particles into the air throughout a city like Providence would not necessarily be detected in the immediate aftermath of the release. Clinical symptoms of inhalational anthrax would not be discovered for at least two or three days after the attack occurred, yet the health effects and environmental consequences could be catastrophic.

Surveillance and Detection Efforts

It is critical to receive warning of a biological attack as soon as it occurs and to identify the causative agent immediately. Such a warning would enable the prevention of most cases of inhalational anthrax through the combined response of the

The Public Health and Economic Systems Are Not Prepared for an Attack

A widespread anthrax attack would pose a serious public health and economic threat to the country. The current public health system has never been forced to deal with such an attack, and it is questionable whether, in its current state, it could be effective. In addition, a terrorist attack would have a crippling impact on the economy because there would be widespread panic, people would not be able to go to work, there would be a rush demand for antibiotics, and many other disruptions. The full economic impact cannot even be predicted because numerous unforeseen problems would develop. Anthrax is such a potent biological weapon not only because of its innate lethality but also because it poses an immense threat to the economy and the health care system itself. . . .

Given the rarity of anthrax, many physicians are not readily able to recognize the symptoms of anthrax infection. Delay in the first diagnosis will also delay the forensic effort of finding the source of exposure as well as the prophylaxis treatment of people who have been exposed. Anthrax is currently classified as a Category A pathogen for bioweapon purposes by the CDC [Centers for Disease Control and Prevention]. With such a recognizable threat, it is essential for the medical community to be able to identify anthrax immediately and begin the process of treating those who have been exposed. Only then can heavy casualties be avoided after an attack.

Geoffrey Zubay, et al., Agents of Bioterrorism:
Pathogens and Their Weaponization.
New York: Columbia University Press, 2005.

CDC [Centers for Disease Control and Prevention] and its state and local partners in distributing sufficient prophylactic antibiotics to the public before the onset of disease. A delay of just one day in detection of an anthrax release—and therefore treatment of affected populations—would result in thousands of unnecessary deaths.

Sufficient early warning through environmental detection is one of the department's top priorities, one for which the Office of Health Affairs, working with the Science and Technology Directorate (S&T), is responsible. We are investing significant amounts of taxpayer resources to our BioWatch program, which provides detection and warning of a biological attack in our nation's highest risk urban areas through a series of pathogen detectors. With S&T, we are developing the next generation of detectors, known as Generation 3, which will be automated and significantly reduce detection time to allow our health providers to get countermeasures into the hands of affected populations within the critical window of time to save lives.

Complementing our BioWatch capabilities is our establishment of a robust biosurveillance integration center, where other departments and agencies come together to monitor their biological data and analyze potential biological threats. The National Biosurveillance Integration Center (NBIC), authorized in the 9/11 Act (P.L. 110-53), will bring together data from other federal departments, the public domain and eventually the private sector and states and local government to understand and characterize biological events and incidents across the areas of human health, animal health, food, water, and the environment. Through robust data analysis and integration across these sectors, we aim to provide the earliest possible warning of outbreaks and threats to human and veterinary health and the food and water supply. Over the past several months, we have made great progress in our governance structure. We now have all the relevant departments coming to an "ownership meeting," which recognizes that DHS [Department of Homeland Security] is the host for NBIC, but the system belongs to every department across the federal government that needs access to a biosurveillance common operating picture (BCOP). We are working very closely with the CDC as . . . [it] develops improved human health surveillance systems, which will be a vital element of the government's BCOP. It is in all of our interests to ensure the success of our partner agencies' improvements in their data systems.

Federal, State, and Local Response and Recovery

If a large-scale biological attack occurred here in downtown Providence using aerosolized anthrax, it would likely go undetected for days, until large numbers of people begin showing up in emergency departments and doctors' offices two to five days after the attack. Unfortunately, most cases would progress quickly to a form of pneumonia that is very resistant to treatment once it has started. The sentinel cases would be those receiving the highest doses of anthrax spores, and would be the harbinger of tens of thousands more, nearly all requiring intensive medical care, including ventilatory support and the anthrax countermeasures we have in the Strategic National Stockpile (SNS). Federal, state, and local law enforcement would seek to identify the perpetrators to prevent subsequent attacks. Since we do not know the extent of the exposure, federal and local health officials would likely mobilize the SNS for antibiotics to be given to the population as environmental sensors and samples identify the affected areas. In such a scenario, state and local resources, including medical assets, would be taxed if not overwhelmed. Rather than a smoking building defining the extent of the victims, every man, woman, and child in the area—and every building and every farm in the plume—could be affected. This is not a pretty picture, so preparedness is required to minimize the impact. . . .

The threat of bioterrorism against the U.S. remains a significant concern. We continue to face an enemy determined to acquire and develop biological agents into weapons of mass destruction against the homeland. The Office of Health Affairs and the Department of Homeland Security take this threat very seriously and are doing significant work to prevent, enhance early detection and surveillance and integrate federal, state and local preparedness and response capabilities to reduce the catastrophic consequences of a biological attack on the homeland.

> *"While anthrax does form hardy spores that can remain inert for a period of time, the disease is not easily transmitted from person to person, and therefore is unlikely to create an epidemic outside of the area targeted by the attack."*

Anthrax Is Not a Serious Threat

Fred Burton and Scott Stewart

In the following viewpoint, Fred Burton and Scott Stewart maintain that anthrax is not the catastrophic threat that it has been portrayed to be. Although terrorist groups such as al Qaeda have demonstrated an interest in using biological weapons against the United States, and an anthrax attack could be harmful and disruptive, the authors argue that the actual effective weaponizing of anthrax is problematic and well beyond the capability of terrorists groups. Burton and Stewart are contributing columnists for Stratfor Global Intelligence.

Fred Burton and Scott Stewart, "Busting the Anthrax Myth," STRATFOR Global Intelligence, July 30, 2008. Copyright © STRATFOR 2009. www.stratfor.com. Republished with permission.

As you read, consider the following questions:

1. What is one of the three most common misconceptions involving biological weapons, according to the authors?

2. According to Fred Burton and Scott Stewart, anthrax can be deadly if inhaled; is it also deadly if it comes in contact with a person's skin?

3. In the authors' opinion, how difficult is it to obtain a biological agent?

D r. Jeffrey W. Runge, chief medical officer at the U.S. Department of Homeland Security, told a congressional subcommittee on July 22 [2008] that the risk of a large-scale biological attack on the nation is significant and that the U.S. government knows its terrorist enemies have sought to use biological agents as instruments of warfare. Runge also said that the United States believes that capability is within the terrorists' reach. . . .

We do not disagree with Runge's statements that actors such as al Qaeda have demonstrated an interest in biological weapons. There is ample evidence that al Qaeda has a rudimentary biological weapons capability. However, there is a huge chasm of capability that separates intent and a rudimentary biological weapons program from a biological weapons program that is capable of killing hundreds of thousands of people.

Misconceptions About Biological Weapons

There are many misconceptions involving biological weapons. The three most common are that they are easy to obtain, that they are easy to deploy effectively, and that, when used, they always cause massive casualties.

While it is certainly true that there are many different types of actors who can easily gain access to rudimentary biological agents, there are far fewer actors who can actually isolate virulent strains of the agents, weaponize them and then effectively employ these agents in a manner that will realistically pose a significant threat of causing mass casualties. While organisms such as anthrax are present in the environment and are not difficult to obtain, more highly virulent strains of these tend to be far more difficult to locate, isolate, and replicate. Such efforts require highly skilled individuals and sophisticated laboratory equipment.

Even incredibly deadly biological substances such as ricin and botulinum toxin are difficult to use in mass attacks. This difficulty arises when one attempts to take a rudimentary biological substance and then convert it into a weaponized form—a form that is potent enough to be deadly and yet readily dispersed. Even if this weaponization hurdle can be overcome, once developed, the weaponized agent must then be integrated with a weapons system that can effectively take large quantities of the agent and evenly distribute it in lethal doses to the intended targets.

During the past several decades in the era of modern terrorism, biological weapons have been used very infrequently and with very little success. This fact alone serves to highlight the gap between the biological warfare misconceptions and reality. Militant groups desperately want to kill people and are constantly seeking new innovations that will allow them to kill larger numbers of people. Certainly if biological weapons were as easily obtained, as easily weaponized, and as effective at producing mass casualties as commonly portrayed, militant groups would have used them far more frequently than they have.

Militant groups are generally adaptive and responsive to failure. If something works, they will use it. If it does not, they will seek more effective means of achieving their deadly goals. A good example of this was the rise and fall of the use of chlorine in militant attacks in Iraq.

Misconceptions About Anthrax

As noted by Runge, the spore-forming bacterium Bacillus anthracis is readily available in nature and can be deadly if inhaled, if ingested or if it comes into contact with a person's skin. What constitutes a deadly dose of inhalation anthrax has not been precisely quantified, but is estimated to be somewhere between 8,000 and 50,000 spores. One gram of weaponized anthrax such as that contained in the letters mailed to U.S. Sens. Tom Daschle and Patrick Leahy in October 2001 can contain up to one trillion spores—enough to cause somewhere between 20 and 100 million deaths. The letters mailed to Daschle and Leahy reportedly contained about one gram each for a total estimated quantity of two grams of anthrax spores: enough to have theoretically killed between 40 and 200 million people. The U.S. Census Bureau estimates that the current population of the United States is 304.7 million. In a worst-case scenario, the letters mailed to Daschle and Leahy theoretically contained enough anthrax spores to kill nearly two-thirds of the U.S. population.

Yet, in spite of their incredibly deadly potential, those letters (along with an estimated five other anthrax letters mailed in a prior wave to media outlets such as the *New York Post* and the major television networks) killed only five people; another 22 victims were infected by the spores but recovered after receiving medical treatment. This difference between the theoretical number of fatal victims—hundreds of millions—and the actual number of victims—five—highlights the challenges in effectively distributing even a highly virulent and weaponized strain of an organism to a large number of potential victims.

To summarize: obtaining a biological agent is fairly simple. Isolating a virulent strain and then weaponizing that strain is somewhat more difficult. But the key to biological warfare—effectively distributing a weaponized agent to the intended target—is the really difficult part of the process. Anyone planning a biological attack against a large target such as a city needs to be concerned about a host of factors such as dilution, wind velocity and direction, particle size and weight, the susceptibility of the disease to ultraviolet light, heat, dryness, or even rain. Small-scale localized attacks such as the 2001 anthrax letters or the 1984 salmonella attack undertaken by the Bhagwan Shree Rajneesh cult are far easier to commit.

It is also important to remember that anthrax is not some sort of untreatable super disease. While anthrax does form hardy spores that can remain inert for a period of time, the disease is not easily transmitted from person to person, and therefore is unlikely to create an epidemic outside of the area targeted by the attack. Anthrax infections can be treated by the use of readily available antibiotics. The spores' incubation period also permits time for early treatment if the attack is noticed.

Past Attempts at Bioterrorism

The deadliest known anthrax incident in recent years occurred in 1979 when an accidental release of aerosolized spores from a Soviet biological weapons facility in Sverdlovsk affected some 94 people—reportedly killing 68 of them. This facility was one of dozens of laboratories that were part of the Soviet Union's massive and well-funded biological weapons program, one that employed thousands of the country's brightest scientists. In fact, it was the largest biological weapons program in history.

Perhaps the largest attempt by a non-state actor to cause mass casualties using anthrax was the series of attacks conducted in 1993 by the Japanese cult group Aum Shinrikyo in Tokyo.

In the late 1980s, Aum's team of trained scientists spent millions of dollars to develop a series of state-of-the-art biological weapons research and production laboratories. The group experimented with botulinum toxin, anthrax, cholera, and Q fever and even tried to acquire the Ebola virus. The group hoped to produce enough biological agent to trigger a global Armageddon. Its first attempts at unleashing mega-death on the world involved the use of botulinum toxin. In April 1990, the group used a fleet of three trucks equipped with aerosol sprayers to release liquid botulinum toxin on targets that included the Imperial Palace, the National Diet of Japan, the U.S. Embassy in Tokyo, two U.S. naval bases and the airport in Narita. In spite of the massive quantities of toxin released, there were no mass casualties, and, in fact, nobody outside of the cult was even aware the attacks had taken place.

When the botulinum operations failed to produce results, Aum's scientists went back to the drawing board and retooled their biological weapons facilities to produce anthrax. By mid-1993, they were ready to launch attacks involving anthrax; between June and August of 1993, the group sprayed thousands of gallons of aerosolized liquid anthrax in Tokyo. This time, Aum not only employed its fleet of sprayer trucks but also used aerosol sprayers mounted on the roof of its headquarters to disperse a cloud of aerosolized anthrax over the city. Again, the attacks produced no results and were not even noticed. It was only after the group's successful 1995 subway attacks using sarin nerve agent that a Japanese government investigation discovered that the 1990 and 1993 biological attacks had occurred.

Difficulties with Biological Weapons Production

Aum Shinrikyo's team of highly trained scientists worked under ideal conditions in a first-world country with a virtually unlimited budget. They were able to travel the world in search of deadly organisms and even received technical advice from former Soviet scientists. The team worked in large, modern laboratory facilities to produce substantial quantities of biological weapons. They were able to operate these facilities in-

"Gross! This isn't anthrax, it's an envelope full of dandruff."

"Gross! This isn't anthrax, it's an envelope full of dandruff." Cartoon by David Cooney. www.CartoonStock.com.

side industrial parks and openly order the large quantities of laboratory equipment they required. Yet, in spite of the millions of dollars the group spent on its biological weapons program—and the lack of any meaningful interference from the Japanese government—Aum still experienced problems in creating virulent biological agents and also found it difficult to dispense those agents effectively.

Today, al Qaeda finds itself operating in a very different environment than that experienced by Aum Shinrikyo in 1993. At that time, nobody was looking for Aum or its biological and chemical weapons program. By contrast, since the Sept. 11 [2001 terrorist] attacks, the United States and its allies have actively pursued al Qaeda leaders and sought to dismantle and defang the organization. The United States and its allies have focused a considerable amount of resources in tracking and disassembling al Qaeda's chemical and biological warfare efforts. The al Qaeda network has had millions of dollars of its assets seized in a number of countries, and it no longer has the safe haven of Afghanistan from which to operate. The chemical and biological facilities the group established in the 1990s in Afghanistan—such as the Deronta training camp, where cyanide and other toxins were used to kill dogs, and a crude anthrax production facility in Kandahar—have been found and destroyed by U.S. troops.

Operating in the badlands along the Pakistani-Afghan border, al Qaeda cannot easily build large modern factories capable of producing large quantities of agents or toxins. Such fixed facilities are expensive and consume a lot of resources. Even if al Qaeda had the spare capacity to invest in such facilities, the fixed nature of them means that they could be compromised and quickly destroyed by the United States.

If al Qaeda could somehow create and hide a fixed biological weapons facility in Pakistan's Federally Administered Tribal Areas or North-West Frontier Province, it would still face the daunting task of transporting large quantities of biological agents from the Pakistani badlands to targets in the United States or Europe. Al Qaeda operatives certainly can create and transport small quantities of these compounds, but not enough to wreak the kind of massive damage it desires.

Al Qaeda's lead chemical and biological weapons expert, Midhat Mursi al-Sayid Umar, also known as Abu Khabab al-Masri, was reportedly killed on July 28, 2008, by a U.S. missile strike on his home in Pakistan. Al-Sayid, who had a $5 million dollar bounty on his head, was initially reported to have been one of those killed in the January 2006 strike in Damadola. If he was indeed killed, his death should be another significant blow to the group's biological warfare efforts.

Of course, we must recognize that the jihadist threat goes just beyond the al Qaeda core. As we have been writing for several years now, al Qaeda has undergone a metamorphosis from a smaller core group of professional operatives into an operational model that encourages independent grassroots jihadists to conduct attacks. The core al Qaeda group, through men like al-Sayid, has published manuals in hard copy and on the Internet that provide instructions on how to manufacture rudimentary biological weapons.

It is our belief that independent jihadist cells and lone-wolf jihadists will almost certainly attempt to brew up some of the recipes from the al Qaeda cookbook. There also exists a very real threat that a jihadist sympathizer could obtain a small quantity of deadly biological organisms by infiltrating a research facility.

This means that we likely will see some limited attempts at employing biological weapons. That does not mean, however, that such attacks will be large-scale or create mass casualties.

Ineffectiveness of Bioterrorism

While there has been much consternation and alarm-raising over the potential for widespread proliferation of biological weapons and the possible use of such weapons on a massive scale, there are significant constraints on such designs. The current dearth of substantial biological weapons programs and arsenals by governments worldwide, and the even smaller number of cases in which systems were actually used, seems to belie—or at least bring into question—the intense concern about such programs.

While we would like to believe that countries such as the United States, the United Kingdom, and Russia have halted their biological warfare programs for some noble ideological or humanitarian reason, we simply can't. If biological weapons were in practice as effective as some would lead us to believe, these states would surely maintain stockpiles of them, just as they have maintained their nuclear weapons programs. Biological weapons programs were abandoned because they proved to be not as effective as advertised and because conventional munitions proved to provide more bang for the buck.

In some ways, the psychological fear of a "super weapon"—undetectable, microscopic, easily delivered and extremely deadly—shapes assessment of the threat, more so than an objective understanding of actual capability and intent (not to mention the extreme difficulties of ever creating some sort of a super bug). Conventional weapons systems, and unconventional tactics, continue to be the most cost-effective and proven methods of warfare, whether between state actors or between state and non-state actors. Nuclear weapons have also been shown to have true weapons of mass destruction power.

To help keep the cost-benefit calculation of a biological warfare program in perspective, consider that Seung-Hui Cho, the man who committed the shooting at Virginia Tech [in 2007], killed 32 people—more than six times as many as were killed by the 2001 anthrax letters. John Mohammed, the so-called "D.C. Sniper," was able to cause a considerable amount of panic and kill twice as many people (10) by simply purchasing and using one assault riffle [in 2002]. Compare Mohammed's effort and expenses to that of the Aum Shinrikyo anthrax program that took years of work by a huge team and millions of dollars to develop but infected no one.

Level of Concern Regarding Biological Weapons

Now, just because biological weapons are not all they are cracked up to be does not mean that efforts to undermine the biological warfare plans and efforts of militant groups such as al Qaeda should not continue or that programs to detect such agents or develop more effective treatments and vaccines should be halted. Even though an anthrax attack probably will not kill huge numbers of people, as we saw in the case of the anthrax letters, such an attack can be quite disruptive. Cleaning up after such an attack is expensive and takes considerable time and effort. Like a dirty bomb, an anthrax attack will more likely serve as a weapon of mass disruption and not a weapon of mass destruction.

Due to the disruption and the potential for some deaths as a result of an anthrax attack, the threat against the United States does remain a significant concern. However, the threat it represents is not as great as that of conventional attacks using firearms and explosives against soft targets, and it certainly does not rise anywhere near the level of a threat posed by a terrorist attack using a nuclear weapon.

Homeland security resources are very limited and have been shrinking as we move further from 9/11 [2001] and as other items begin to take precedence in the federal budget. This means that an array of different programs is being forced to scramble for an ever-shrinking piece of the funding pie. In such an environment, it is often a temptation to overstate the threat. Such overstatements are harmful because they can sometimes prevent a rational distribution of resources and prevent resources from being allocated to where they are needed most.

> "Unfortunately, the possibility of releas-
> ing smallpox in aerosolized form is now
> a reality and the potential for a cata-
> strophic scenario is great, and effective
> control measures must be imple-
> mented."

Smallpox Remains a Bioterrorism Threat

Stefan Riedel

*Stefan Riedel, an assistant professor at Johns Hopkins Bayview
Medical Center, has written numerous articles about infectious
diseases and bacterial resistance. In the following viewpoint, he
explains how smallpox came to be eradicated in 1977, but notes
that stocks of the virus are still kept in laboratories for research
despite calls for worldwide destruction of the virus. Riedel contends that because smallpox is highly contagious and results in
high mortality rates, it has the potential to be used as a biological weapon.*

Stefan Riedel, "Smallpox and Biological Warfare: A Disease Revisited," *Baylor University
Medical Center Proceedings*, vol. 18, January 2005, pp. 13–14, 17–19. Reproduced by permission.

As you read, consider the following questions:

1. Smallpox is considered a Category A bioterrorism agent by the Centers for Disease Control and Prevention. According to Stefan Riedel, what does that signify?

2. According to Riedel, why did the World Health Assembly recommend in 1980 that all countries cease vaccinations against smallpox?

3. In the author's viewpoint, what would be a reason to recommend widespread smallpox vaccination?

Smallpox is one of the most devastating diseases that could potentially be used as a biological weapon. In fact, smallpox was for many centuries devastating to mankind. However, the remarkable efforts of the World Health Organization led to its eradication in 1977. With the developments in more recent years, the threat of biological and chemical warfare has reemerged. In particular, the events surrounding the attack on the World Trade Center on September 11, 2001, as well as the recent developments in Afghanistan and the Middle East, have shown that the threat of biological weapons is real and present in today's time.

The Centers for Disease Control and Prevention (CDC) in Atlanta [Georgia] has classified various organisms and diseases that could potentially be used as biological weapons. These diseases are grouped in three categories according to their possibility of use and their impact on public health. Smallpox is listed in group A, indicating that it is easily disseminated and transmitted from person to person and results in high mortality rates. . . .

A Brief History of Smallpox

Smallpox was introduced to Europe sometime between the fifth and seventh centuries and was frequently epidemic during the Middle Ages. Smallpox continued to be a problem throughout the 17th and 18th centuries, affecting populations on a large scale. Variolation was a semi-effective measure to prevent the disease; however, the procedure was not without risk. With Edward Jenner's demonstration in 1796 that inoculation with cowpox provided protection against smallpox, the potential threat of the disease was greatly diminished. The procedure of vaccination, as Jenner named it, was rapidly introduced in England, Europe, and North America. In later years, it was also introduced in many of the other European colonies. . . .

The threat of smallpox being used as a biological weapon in war was greatly diminished when a large part of the European population was vaccinated. However, during the second half of the 19th century, it was realized that vaccination did not confer lifelong immunity and that subsequent revaccination was necessary. The mortality from smallpox had declined, but the regular occurrence of epidemics indicated that the disease was still not under control. In the 1950s many countries implemented various control measures, and smallpox was finally eradicated in many areas in Europe and North America.

The process of worldwide eradication of smallpox was set in motion when the World Health Assembly received a report in 1958 of the catastrophic consequences of smallpox in 63 countries, mostly in Asia and Africa. In 1967, a global campaign was begun under the guardianship of the World Health Organization (WHO), which finally succeeded in eradicating smallpox in 1977. On May 8, 1980, the World Health Assembly announced that the world was free of smallpox and recommended that all countries cease vaccination.

A WHO expert committee recommended the worldwide destruction of stocks of variola virus in all laboratories. Two reference laboratories were said to retain stocks of the virus for future research: the Institute of Virus Preparations in Moscow, Russia, and the CDC in Atlanta, Georgia. All countries reported compliance in 1981. The WHO committee later recommended that all virus stocks be destroyed by June 1999, and the 1996 World Health Assembly concurred with this decision. In 1998, an expert committee of the Institute of Medicine concluded that continuing and future research on the variola virus was needed and that the virus should be retained at the two approved facilities. The WHO expert panel agreed to these recommendations. The virus is still kept at the approved facilities in Moscow and Atlanta.

More recently, allegations brought forth by Ken Alibek, a former deputy director of the Former Soviet Union's bioweapons program, have raised concerns among Western countries that smallpox could be used as a biological weapon. According to Alibek, the Former Soviet Union expanded its bioweapons research program during the 1980s and was eventually able to weaponize smallpox. This research was conducted at remote facilities in Siberia. However, very little information is available about the extent and outcome of this research and where it was conducted. Since the financial support for Russian laboratories has substantially declined in recent years, there are increasing concerns that the existing expertise and equipment might fall into non-Russian hands. With the recently increasing terrorist activities worldwide, the concerns raised in the late 1990s become more real. . . .

Preventive Measures Against Smallpox

Before 1972, smallpox vaccination was recommended for all children in Europe and the USA at age 1 year. Most countries and most US states also required that the child be revaccinated before school entry. Special recommendations existed for military personnel and for tourists planning to visit certain foreign countries. Routine vaccinations in the USA were stopped in 1972, and since then few persons younger than 30 years have been vaccinated. The duration of protective immunity from previous vaccinations was historically based on the experience of naturally exposed susceptible persons. However, this has never been satisfactorily evaluated. Therefore, the world population is now considered an immunologically naïve, nonprotected population, highly susceptible to smallpox, should the disease be reintroduced.

Worldwide only a small supply of smallpox vaccine is available. Most of this supply is under the control of the CDC; additional doses of vaccine are available at the WHO. The USA is currently increasing the number of doses of smallpox vaccine. . . .

Efforts to develop and produce a new vaccine are now focused on a live cell culture-derived smallpox vaccine. In 2001, it was estimated that the development and licensure of such a vaccine as well as development of a production facility would require a minimum of 36 months. Since only a limited amount of vaccine is available, the Advisory Committee on Immunization Practices recommended in 2001 that a preventive vaccination program be initiated to protect the first-line responders, i.e., emergency and key health care personnel and law enforcement personnel. Such newly vaccinated persons also should receive a booster dose every 10 years, as recommended by the committee. Currently, widespread vaccination is recommended only under epidemic circumstances, in the event of a laboratory accident or an act of bioterrorism. . . .

In the situation of a clandestine release of smallpox, even if only 50 to 100 people were infected at first, the disease would rapidly spread in a now highly susceptible population, expanding by a factor of 10 to 20 times with each generation of cases. As soon as the diagnosis of smallpox is established, all individuals in whom the disease is suspected should be isolated immediately. Close contacts such as household members should be vaccinated and placed under surveillance for disease symptoms.

Smallpox transmission within hospitals has long been recognized as a serious problem. For more than 200 years, smallpox patients were cared for in specialized hospitals to minimize the spread of the disease. In the setting of a limited outbreak with few cases, patients could be admitted to hospitals and confined to rooms under negative pressure and equipped with high-efficiency particulate air filtration. Since smallpox in aerosolized form can be easily disseminated and poses a serious threat in hospitals and public places, different guidelines exist for large smallpox outbreaks, and patients should then be isolated in their homes or other non-hospital facilities. According to the recommendations of the Advisory Committee on Immunization Practices and the Working Group on Civilian Biodefense, home care seems to be a reasonable approach, since little can be done for the patient other than to offer supportive care. In addition, antibiotics may be indicated for treatment of occasional secondary bacterial infections.

Containment of Smallpox Outbreaks

No antiviral substances have the proven potential to be effective in the treatment of human smallpox infection. Therefore, the strategy for control of a smallpox outbreak centers on surveillance and containment. This strategy was instrumental in the global eradication of smallpox in the past century. An assessment algorithm [procedure for solving a problem] devised by the CDC can help in identifying smallpox in a febrile patient with a rash. This algorithm can be obtained from state health departments or online from the CDC. Identification and surveillance of the individual's close contacts are the center of every proposed strategy of disease containment. Priority within the rings of contact will be determined by interviews with the patients and their contacts. Surveillance and vaccination should begin as soon as those contacts are identified. Vaccination within 4 days after exposure is currently considered effective in preventing infection or the severe form of infection. Vaccinated contacts are not considered infective and do

Like a Nuclear War

Biological weapons are among the most dangerous in the world today and can be engineered and disseminated to achieve a more deadly result than a nuclear attack. Whereas the explosion of a nuclear bomb would cause massive death in a specific location, a biological attack with smallpox could infect multitudes of people across the globe. With incubation periods of up to 17 days, human disseminators could unwittingly cause widespread exposure before diagnosable symptoms indicate an infection and appropriate quarantine procedures are in place.

Unlike any other type of weapon, bioweapons such as smallpox can replicate and infect a chain of people over an indeterminate amount of time from a single undetectable point of release. According to science writer and author of *The Hot Zone*, Richard Preston, "If you took a gram of smallpox, which is highly contagious and lethal, and for which there's no vaccine available globally now, and released it in the air and created about a hundred cases, the chances are excellent that the virus would go global in six weeks as people moved from city to city. . . . The death toll could easily hit the hundreds of millions. . . . In scale, that's like a nuclear war."

Janet Ellen Levy, "The Threat of Bioweapons,"
American Thinker, *June 8, 2007.*

not have to be isolated. However, it is currently recommended that they stay within 20 miles of their home.

In addition to hospital infection control and the containment of identified cases, decontamination of the environment after an attack with aerosolized smallpox is an important factor to control the spread of the disease. If vaccinia virus is released as aerosol and not exposed to ultraviolet light, it may persist for as long as 24 hours or somewhat longer under favorable conditions. It is believed that variola virus would exhibit similar properties. However, by the time the first cases of smallpox become clinically evident, no viable smallpox virus would be present in the environment. Virus identified in scabs appears to be more durable, and survival of up to 8 weeks depending on temperature conditions has been observed. Therefore, special focus should be given to the close environment of patients. The occurrence of smallpox infections among personnel who handled laundry from infected patients is well documented. It is believed that virus remains viable for much longer periods, requiring special precautions and procedures for handling such material from infected patients. . . .

The Potential Danger of Smallpox

Although smallpox was eradicated in 1980, it remains a potential agent of biowarfare and bioterrorism. It is considered a Category A organism, which is easy to disseminate and transmit from person to person. Furthermore, smallpox has the potential to result in high mortality rates with a major public health impact, eventually causing public panic and social disruption. Given the enormous efforts made to eradicate the disease, the deliberate release of smallpox as a biological weapon would be an international crime of unprecedented proportions. Unfortunately, the possibility of releasing smallpox in aerosolized form is now a reality and the potential for a catastrophic scenario is great, and effective control measures must be implemented.

Many models have been developed for emergency response. However, all leave many uncertainties, and no model can be truly predictive in the context of smallpox outbreak planning. But it is clear from reviewing different scenarios that early detection, isolation of infected individuals, surveillance of contacts, and a focused, selective vaccination program are the essential items of an effective control program.

The efficacy of such a program, however, depends on the level of education, both in the public as well as in the medical community. Education of health care professionals should permit early detection of infected individuals and allow for prompt initiation of adequate first steps to contain the approaching epidemic. Advanced planning for isolation of infected individuals, both in their homes as well as in hospitals, will be critical to prevent the outbreak from further expansion. Finally, the success in conquering the threat of a reemerging smallpox epidemic will rest on the availability of adequate supplies of vaccine and other medications necessary for treatment. To ensure an effective and relatively inexpensive safeguard for such a tragedy, it is necessary to provide an adequate stockpile of vaccine. However, proper education of the medical community as well as the public remains an essential cornerstone of such preventive efforts.

Periodical Bibliography

The following articles have been selected to supplement the diverse views presented in this chapter.

Pushpa M. Bhargava	"The Growing Planetary Threat from Biological Weapons and Terrorism," *Tribune* (India), November 30, 2008.
Delaware Criminal Justice Council	"Biological Threats and Bioterrorism," March 2007. http://cjc.delaware.gov.
eMedicineHealth	"Smallpox," October 31, 2005. www.emedicine health.com.
Liudvikas Jagminas	"Evaluation of a Biological Warfare Victim," eMedicine, July 11, 2008. www.eMedicine.com.
Mary T. Johnson	"Anthrax, Biological Weapons, and Bioterrorism," Terre Haute School of Medicine, Indiana University, April 23, 2008.
Paul Kerr	"Nuclear, Biological, and Chemical Weapons and Missiles: Status and Trends," Congressional Research Service, February 20, 2008.
Alex Kingsbury	"Slew of Warnings on Nuclear, Biological Terrorism Prompt Worries of Fearmongering," *U.S. News & World Report*, March 29, 2009.
Janet Ellen Levy	"The Threat of Bioweapons," *American Thinker*, June 8, 2007.
Wendy Orent	"Crying Wolf over Bioterrorism," *Los Angeles Times*, March 2, 2008.
Claude Salhani	"Worse than Nuclear Threat," *Washington Times*, July 10, 2008.

CHAPTER 2

Who Constitutes
a Serious Biological
Warfare Threat?

Chapter Preface

When the subject of terrorism is mentioned, many Americans think of the four commercial jetliners that were hijacked on September 11, 2001—the deadliest terrorist attack on United States soil. Osama bin Laden, al Qaeda, or another foreign extremist group might also come to mind. The second deadliest act of terrorism in the United States, however, was the bombing of the Alfred P. Murrah Federal Building in Oklahoma City by American citizens Timothy McVeigh and Terry Nichols on April 19, 1995. In fact, between 1980 and 2000, 250 of the 335 acts of terrorism in the United States were carried out by America's own citizens, according to the Federal Bureau of Investigation. The phenomenon is termed "domestic terrorism," and it has become an area of increasing national concern.

On April 7, 2009, the United States Department of Homeland Security distributed a "for-official-use-only" report to counterterrorism and law enforcement officials that assessed the likelihood of domestic right-wing extremist groups carrying out terrorist attacks against the United States. The report, titled "Rightwing Extremism: Current Economic and Political Climate Fueling Resurgence in Radicalization and Recruitment," broadly defined right-wing extremists as "groups, movements, and adherents that are primarily hate-oriented (based on hatred of particular religious, racial, or ethnic groups), and those [groups] that are mainly antigovernment, rejecting federal authority. . . . It may include groups and individuals that are dedicated to a single issue such as opposition to abortion or immigration." Of particular concern is that these American extremists are being targeted as potential recruits for al Qaeda to carry out biological warfare or other forms of terrorist attacks. Counterterrorism officials have reported an intensified al Qaeda outreach to Westerners, which includes videos and Web sites in English. One authenticated video specifically suggests that al Qaeda make "common cause" with three hundred thousand members of white supremacist and other militias in the United States. The speaker in the video, known terrorist and al Qaeda associate Abdullah al-Nafisi, says, "Four pounds of anthrax—in a suitcase this big—carried by a fighter through tunnels from Mexico into the United States are guaranteed to kill 330,000 Americans within a single hour if it is properly spread in population centers there."

The Department of Defense and the Department of Homeland Security are also scrutinizing activities and studies being conducted in various biodefense research laboratories located throughout the United States. Researchers in some of these facilities actually create virulent disease agents—in essence, bioweapons—to learn how to defend against them. Many government officials, public health professionals, social scientists, and citizens have expressed concern regarding the lack of safety and security regulations encompassing these laboratories and the access a potential terrorist or rogue scientist has to lethal pathogens. A case in point is Bruce E. Ivins, the American biodefense scientist who allegedly sent letters containing anthrax spores to several news media offices and two United States senators in 2001. In addition to causing widespread panic, the infected letters killed five people, sickened at least seventeen others, crippled the national mail service, and cost the nation over $1 billion to decontaminate postal facilities and government buildings.

While the terrorist threat from foreign extremist groups and rogue nations is significant, the counterterrorism community recognizes that the threat from domestic terrorists is also significant and should not be ignored. As Laura H. Kahn wrote in her 2008 article "Biosecurity Lessons from the Bruce Ivins Case" for the *Bulletin of the Atomic Scientists*, "The most dangerous bioterrorism threat we face is from ourselves." In this chapter, experts analyze some of the leading nations and groups that might also be pursuing the use of biological warfare.

"*Transnational and domestic terrorists and state sponsors of terrorism continue to demonstrate an interest in acquiring and using chemical, biological, radiological, and nuclear weapons.*"

Foreign and Domestic Terrorist Groups Are a Serious Biological Warfare Threat

Robert S. Mueller III

In the following testimony before the U.S. Senate Select Committee on Intelligence, Robert S. Mueller III, director of the Federal Bureau of Investigation (FBI), explains that foreign terrorist groups such as al Qaeda are intent on attacking the United States, possibly with the use of chemical or biological weapons. He further maintains that several radical political and religious groups existing within the United States plan to conduct attacks on national targets utilizing a variety of tactics, including explosive devices and biological weapons.

Robert S. Mueller III, "Congressional Testimony: Statement Before the Senate Select Committee on Intelligence," January 11, 2007. www.fbi.gov.

As you read, consider the following questions:

1. Robert S. Mueller III contends that al Qaeda's focus of attacks includes "soft targets." What is an example of a soft target?

2. What communication forum has facilitated the ability of al Qaeda sympathizers to spread their extremist propaganda, according to Mueller?

3. Why is it difficult to infiltrate and detect the actions of domestic animal rights extremist and eco-terrorism groups, according to the author?

In 2006, successes in the war on terrorism and the arrests of many key al Qaeda leaders and operatives have diminished the ability of the group to attack the United States homeland. At the same time, the growing Sunni extremist movement that al Qaeda successfully spearheaded has evolved from being directly led by al Qaeda to a global jihadi [religious warriors] movement that is able to conduct attacks independently.

As a result, the United States homeland faces two very different threats from international terrorism: the attack planning that continues to emanate from core al Qaeda overseas and the threat posed by homegrown, self-radicalizing groups and individuals—inspired, but not led by al Qaeda—who are already living in the U.S. While they share a similar ideology, these two groups pose vastly different threats due to their differences in intent and attack capability.

Assessing the Threat from al Qaeda

The United States has made significant headway in countering al Qaeda's ability to execute attacks worldwide, including the U.S. homeland, but the group continues to pose the most serious international terrorism threat we face.

Despite the successes this year [2007] in depleting al Qaeda's senior ranks and disrupting ongoing attack planning, the group has been able to rebuild itself and remain viable—finding new staging grounds for attacks, promoting from within, and using the skills and abilities of its seasoned veterans to continue its worldwide attack planning.

We assess al Qaeda's strategy for conducting an attack inside the United States continues to include proven tactics and tradecraft with adaptations designed to address its losses and our enhanced security measures.

For example, we believe:

- Al Qaeda is still seeking to infiltrate operatives into the U.S. from overseas who have no known nexus to terrorism using both legal and possibly illegal methods of entry.

- We also believe, if it can, al Qaeda will obtain and use some form of chemical, biological, radiological, or nuclear material.

- Al Qaeda's choice of targets and attack methods will most likely continue to focus on economic targets such as aviation, the energy sector, and mass transit; soft targets such as large public gatherings; and symbolic targets such as monuments and government buildings.

Throughout 2006, al Qaeda made efforts to align itself with established regional terrorist groups such as the Salafist Group for Preaching and Combat, or GSPC, that may expand the scope of the threat to the homeland. In addition, al Qaeda is also finding it easy to attract individual members of these groups who align closer to [founder Osama] Bin Laden's ideology and crave a more global agenda. This strategy has been particularly successful in recruiting individuals from Pakistani and Kashmiri militant groups operating overseas, as was evident in the recently disrupted al Qaeda–related airline plot out of the United Kingdom.

Comparing Threats Against the United States and the United Kingdom

In a recent [August 2006] and rare public statement by the director of the British Security Service [BSS], Eliza Manningham-Buller outlined the terrorist threat the United Kingdom is currently facing and cited some sobering statistics that highlighted the continuing threat to the U.S. and its allies. According to the BSS director, the United Kingdom is tracking 1,600 individuals who are part of at least 200 networks that are actively plotting terrorist attacks against British targets, as well as Western targets overseas. She added the United Kingdom is following at least 30 plots as of November 2006, many of which are linked to al Qaeda in Pakistan and using British-born foot soldiers living in the United Kingdom in its attack planning.

Due to the stark differences in the history, the population, and the immigrant assimilation in our two countries, it is difficult to directly compare our terrorism threat to theirs. While in general, the number of subjects we are monitoring is proportional to the number of subjects BSS is monitoring—based on gross national population—we see relatively fewer active "plots" involving physical attacks within the United States, less defined networks of extremists, and less developed attack planning compared to those described by the BSS director.

It is also possible, however, that al Qaeda's strategy for attacking the U.S. homeland includes using the U.K. as a stepping stone for al Qaeda operatives to enter the United States. We are working closely with our partners in the United Kingdom to counter this possible threat and to identify any U.S. connections to the U.K. networks currently being monitored.

Examining the Homegrown Threat

As I stated earlier, we face two different threats from international terrorism. And when we look at the homegrown threat, in contrast to the threat from al Qaeda, it is critical to be aware of the differences in intent and capability in order to understand and counter the threat. This year [2007], we disrupted several unsophisticated, small-scale attack plans that reflect the broader problem homegrown extremists pose.

Last year [2006], we disrupted a homegrown Sunni Islamic extremist group in California known as the JIS, a.k.a. "Assembly of Authentic Islam," operating primarily in state prisons, without apparent connections or direction from outside the United States and no identifiable foreign nexus. Members of the JIS committed armed robberies in Los Angeles with the goal of financing terrorist attacks against the enemies of Islam, including the U.S. government and supporters of Israel.

This past summer, we arrested Narseal Batiste, the leader of a group with intentions to wage jihad against the United States and that was seeking to create its own army and government. Batiste also recognized his resource limitations and sought to obtain material support or take direction from al Qaeda. The group was composed mostly of U.S. persons, many of them born in the United States, and their intentions were to attack inside this country.

Also in 2006, the FBI, along with other federal agencies and foreign partners, dismantled a global network of extremists operating primarily on the Internet and independently of any known terrorist organization. The leaders of this group, who were from Georgia, had long-term goals of creating a large network of extremists in preparation for conducting attacks, possibly inside the U.S.

The diversity of homegrown extremists and the direct knowledge they have of the United States makes the threat they pose potentially very serious. The radicalization of U.S. Muslim converts is of particular concern. While conversion to Islam in itself does not directly lead to radicalization, converts appear to be more vulnerable and likely to be placed in situations that put them in a position to be influenced by Islamic extremists.

Spreading Terrorist Propaganda

In 2006, al Qaeda and its sympathizers continued their attempts to make global jihad accessible to English-speaking Western Muslims by disseminating large amounts of violent Islamic extremist propaganda in English via media outlets and the Internet. Multiple Internet sites that are dedicated to the spread of radical Islamic propaganda deftly exploited any and all terrorist and political events, including the war in Iraq.

Al-Sahab, al Qaeda's official media component, released 48 videos last year, the most al Qaeda ever released in one year. This acceleration in production is likely intended to mobilize the global jihad movement and demonstrate that al Qaeda remains relevant and its main ideological driver.

The Internet has facilitated the radicalization process, particularly in the United States, by providing access to a broad and constant stream of extremist Islamic propaganda, as well as experienced and possibly well-connected operators via Web forums and chat rooms. . . .

Understanding the Threat from Domestic Terrorist Groups

While much of the national attention is focused on the substantial threat posed by international terrorists to the homeland, we must also contend with an ongoing threat posed by domestic terrorists based and operating strictly within the United States. Domestic terrorists, motivated by a number of political or social issues, continue to use violence and criminal activity to further their agendas.

Despite the fragmentation of white supremacist groups resulting from the deaths or the arrests of prominent leaders,

An Enemy with No National Boundaries

Regarding the use of biological agents by governments, a form of "protection" is already in place. One question remaining from the Gulf War is why Iraq chose not to use its extensive biological arsenal against U.S. troops. One theory, among many, is that they feared an even greater reprisal, perhaps nuclear. When planning retaliation against a specific country, a nation like the United States could focus on defined military installations, cities, and other targets. Terrorist organizations, however, are not confined to national boundaries, nor do they have defined locations at which a country could direct retaliation. Terrorist organizations are by definition stateless entities; they have members dispersed throughout the world, and it can be difficult if not impossible to completely eliminate their threat. How can one strike back against an enemy that does not have an address? The U.S. "War on Terrorism," specifically the attempts to destroy all remnants of al Qaeda and capture Osama bin Laden, highlights the difficulty in waging a war against a terrorist organization that does not adhere to national boundaries.

Geoffrey Zubay, et al.,
Agents of Bioterrorism: Pathogens and Their Weaponization.
New York: Columbia University Press, 2005.

violence from this element remains an ongoing threat to government targets, Jewish individuals and establishments, and non-white ethnic groups.

The militia/sovereign citizen movement similarly continues to present a threat to law enforcement and members of the judiciary. Members of these groups will continue to intimidate and sometimes threaten judges, prosecutors, and other officers of the court. Sporadic incidents resulting in direct clashes with law enforcement are possible and will most likely involve state and local law enforcement personnel such as highway patrol officers and sheriffs' deputies.

Some U.S.-based black separatist groups follow radical variants of Islam and in some cases express solidarity with international terrorist groups. These groups could utilize black separatists to collect intelligence on U.S. targets or to identify radical elements within the African American community who could act as surrogates on their behalf.

Animal rights extremism and eco-terrorism continue to pose a threat. Extremists within these movements generally operate in small, autonomous cells and employ strict operational security tactics making detection and infiltration difficult. These extremists utilize a variety of tactics, including arson, vandalism, animal theft, and the use of explosive devices.

Acquiring Weapons of Mass Destruction

Transnational and domestic terrorists and state sponsors of terrorism continue to demonstrate an interest in acquiring and using chemical, biological, radiological, and nuclear weapons, or CBRN. CBRN weapons are advantageous for terrorists to use to cause mass casualties, mass panic, economic disruption, and summon U.S. government responses.

Few if any terrorist groups are likely to have the capability to produce complex biological or chemical agents needed for a mass casualty attack, but their capability will improve as they pursue enhancing their scientific knowledge base by recruiting scientists as some groups are doing. Currently, terrorist groups have access to simple chemical and biological agent recipes passed on at training camps or through the Internet and anarchist cookbook publications.

Although a nuclear terrorist attack is the least likely to occur due to the required technical expertise and challenges associated with acquiring weapons-usable material, the intent of terrorists to obtain this material is a continuing concern. The ability of a terrorist group to build and use a radiological dispersal device is well within the capability of extremists who already understand explosives if they are able to acquire radiological material.

To counter this threat, the FBI established the WMD [weapons of mass destruction] Directorate in July 2006 to consolidate the FBI's WMD components. The directorate integrates and links all the necessary intelligence, scientific, and operational components to detect and disrupt the acquisition of WMD capabilities and technologies for use against the U.S. homeland by terrorists and other adversaries.

The U.S. government has identified 21 countries—of which Iran, North Korea, and China are of greatest concern—with the capability to either develop WMD systems or acquire export-controlled WMD and dual-use items and sensitive technologies. The FBI has leveraged its statutory authority in export matters with nexus for foreign counterintelligence activities and enhanced interagency cooperation and coordination to address this threat to U.S. national security.

From an operational perspective, FBI headquarters, field agents, and their counterparts at DHS [Department of Homeland Security] and the Department of Commerce have successfully conducted joint investigations that have led to arrests of individuals for violations of U.S. export laws and have produced intelligence in support of national intelligence collection requirements. The resulting intelligence has enabled the intelligence community to better understand the threat to national security from foreign government exploitation of international commerce in foreign targeting of WMD and other sensitive U.S. technologies and information. . . .

Working closely with our partners in intelligence, law enforcement, military, and diplomatic circles, the FBI's primary responsibility is to neutralize terrorist cells and operatives here in the United States and help dismantle terrorist networks worldwide. Although protecting the United States from terrorist attacks is our first priority, we remain committed to the defense of America against foreign intelligence threats as well as the enforcement of federal criminal laws, all while respecting and defending the Constitution.

| "'*Bioterrorism*' *may or may not develop into a serious concern in the future, but it is* not '*one of the most pressing problems that we have on the planet today.*'"

The Biological Warfare Threat from Terrorist Groups Is Overstated

Milton Leitenberg

Milton Leitenberg asserts in the following viewpoint that the risk and imminence of biological warfare has been deliberately exaggerated. Leitenberg cites U.S. government and military portrayals of biological warfare agents as being extremely lethal in small doses and relatively easy to obtain and weaponize. But according to Leitenberg, a considerable level of expertise is necessary to produce and weaponize biological agents—such as obtaining the appropriate strain of pathogen, handling it correctly, and dispersing the product properly—which no terrorist group is known to possess. Leitenberg is a scholar and an expert on the subject of arms control.

Milton Leitenberg, *Assessing the Biological Weapons and Bioterrorism Threat.* Carlisle, PA: Strategic Studies Institute, December 2005. Reproduced by permission.

As you read, consider the following questions:

1. According to the author, can one kilogram of anthrax kill ninety-five thousand people?

2. In Milton Leitenberg's opinion, did the al Qaeda group that operated in Afghanistan in 2000 and 2001 obtain a pathogenic strain of anthrax?

3. Does the author believe that certain countries have assisted terrorist groups in obtaining biological weapons?

Well before October-November 2001, the spectre of "bio-terrorism" benefited from an extremely successful sales campaign. Between 1995 and 2001, the most common portrayal of the potential for "bioterrorism" was the facile catchphrase, "It's not a matter of whether; just when." This proved to be one of the most successful catchphrases since the old soap powder advertisement, "Duz Does Everything." But, of course, it was a matter of both "whether" and "when," or at least it might have been in this initial period. Those calling for preparation and preventive measures certainly believed, at a minimum, that the imagined sequel to whether and when, ". . . and with what consequences," could be affected. That was the purpose of the wake-up calls. But "whether" and "when" were modifiable also, depending on the policies chosen. It depended most particularly on how the threat was portrayed, and how that portrayal was broadcast to potentially interested parties around the world. Perhaps bioterrorism is a given between whenever "now" is and decades hence, but lots of things can intervene between now and then. The inflated predictions that were common were certainly *not* realistic. Much worse, in addition to being wrong, inflated predictions were counterproductive. They induced interest in BW [biological warfare] in the wrong audiences.

One immediate problem was the conflation of biological weapons and "bioterrorism" (and even between biological "agents" and "weapons"). Biological weapon use had been possible in the entire 20th century. Now the entire subject became subsumed under "bioterrorism." That simple switch in language made it easy to transfer levels of state capability to "terrorists." Everything became and was referred to as "bioterrorism." This wiped out any discrimination, or attempt to discriminate, between the relevant capabilities of state programs and existing terrorist groups as they are known to date. The possibility of incidents involving low numbers of casualties evolved in 2 or 3 years to "mass casualty" terrorism, and in several more years to "Apocalyptic Terrorism." Generic terrorist groups (excluding the perpetrator of the U.S. anthrax events)—none of which had yet shown the ability to master their microbiological ABCs in the real world—were endowed with the prospective ability to genetically engineer pathogens. Yet the resources and capabilities available to states and to terrorist groups are vastly different.

Exaggerating the Capability of Biological Weapons

If we go back 10 years or so, we can look at a series of portrayals of the threat. A 1997 U.S. DoD [Department of Defense] Defense Science Board report grouped the characteristics of both chemical and biological warfare agents:

- They are relatively easy to obtain (certainly compared to nuclear), and potential users do not need access to large and expensive facilities to achieve potent capabilities.

- They can be developed and produced in laboratory or small-scale industrial facilities, which makes them difficult to detect. Also, the technologies required to produce them often have commercial applications as well, so their "dual use" can be plausibly denied.

- They can be extremely lethal, so small quantities can be very effective.

- They can be delivered by a variety of means.

The paragraph went on to add that "a few kilograms of a biological agent could threaten an entire city." Summations of this kind were grossly oversimplified even further. Former secretary of the Navy Richard Danzig's 1997 and 1999 papers contain an example: ". . . a kilogram [of anthrax], depending on meteorological conditions and means of delivery, has the potential to kill hundreds of thousands of people in a metropolitan area . . . biological weapons are so potent and so cheap . . . the technology is readily available . . . so many of our adversaries have biological warfare capabilities. . . ." They do have "the potential," but they might also kill only few, or none at all. More correctly, not 1 kilogram but some 50 kilograms could kill anywhere between 0 and 95,000 people, depending on the initial population number, the quality and nature of the anthrax preparation, the meteorological conditions, and the means of delivery if distributed over a city. More recent model studies by Dean Wilkening at Stanford University have demonstrated the difficulties in releasing biological agents so that they are infective in large airborne releases. The model studies show very wide ranges of variability, over five log units (orders of magnitude).

The years between 1995 and 2000 were characterized, then, by:

- spurious statistics (hoaxes counted as "biological" events);

- unknowable predictions;

- greatly exaggerated consequence estimates;

- gross exaggeration of the feasibility of successfully producing biological agents by non-state actors, except in the case of recruitment of highly experienced professionals, for which there still was no evidence as of 2000;

- the apparent continued absence of a thorough threat assessment; and,

- thoughtless, ill-considered, counterproductive, and extravagant rhetoric.

Nonetheless, these descriptions were considered realistic and taken seriously by people responsible for public safety in various sectors: The director of the World Trade Center in 2001 reported that "what the security people and others were telling us was that the threat was chem-bio. . . . We felt this was the coming wave." He acted on that information, purchasing protective suiting and training programs for his own security personnel. The very day after 9/11 [2001 terrorist attacks], former secretary of defense [William] Cohen predicted that the next attack by al Qaeda would involve biological weapons. There were authoritative assessments during the same period that were substantially different, offering more sophisticated accounts of impediments to successful "bioterrorism." Some of these were made by Colonel David Franz, then deputy commander of USAMRIID [United States Army Medical Research Institute of Infectious Diseases]; John Lauder, then special assistant to the director of Central Intelligence; and Dr. Steven Block, chair of a U.S. DoD Defense Science Board summer study on biological weapons—as well as Dr. Brian Jenkins's critique of "fact-free analysis." All these went by the board after 9/11 and the anthrax events that followed in October and November 2001.

Understanding the Finesse Involved with Biological Weapons

Five essential requirements must be mastered in order to produce biological agents:

- One must obtain the appropriate strain of the disease pathogen.

- One must know how to handle the organism correctly.

- One must know how to grow it in a way that will produce the appropriate characteristics.

- One must know how to store the culture, and to scale up production properly.

- One must know how to disperse the product properly.

A U.S. military field manual dating back to the 1960s remarks on the attributes of a desirable BW agent, that in addition to its pathogenicity, "means must be available for maintaining the agent's virulence or infectivity during production, storage, and transportation." One should add, most particularly during its dispersal as well. Two members of Sweden's biodefense program stress methods on how to optimize formulations of BW agents as the most critical step of all: "The key competence is . . . how to formulate the organisms to facilitate aerosolization of particles that cause severe disease by inhalation."

It is interesting that the classified 1999 DIA [Defense Intelligence Agency] report . . . contained a single sentence regarding the possible use of BW agents by terrorist groups: "Terrorist use should also be anticipated primarily in improvised devices, probably in association with an explosive." No anticipation of the capability for aerosol distribution was mentioned, no overflight of cities, sports stadiums, etc.

In a recent BW "Risk Assessment" published elsewhere, a group of authors from the Sandia National Laboratories listed a series of factors closely paralleling the above as "Technical Hurdles to Successful BW Deployment": acquisition of a virulent agent; production of the agent in suitable form and quantity; and, effective deployment of the agent.

This was summed up in simple words as "obtaining a pathogen or toxin . . . , isolation, amplification, protection against environmental degradation, and development of an effective dissemination method." They concluded that "even a low-consequence event requires a considerable level of expertise to execute." Dr. Steven Block, chair of the U.S. DoD Defense Science Board summer study on biological weapons in the late 1990s explained the same requirements.

> A lesson from the Aum Shinrikyo [a Japanese religious group that attacked Tokyo subways with sarin gas in 1995 after many failed attempts at weaponizing biological agents] case is that any group bent on developing offensive bioweapons capabilities must overcome two significant problems, one biological and the other physical. First, it must acquire and produce stable quantities of a suitably potent agent. For a variety of reasons, this is not the trivial task that it is sometimes made out to be. Second, it must have an effective means of delivering the agent to the intended target. For most, but not all, bioweapon agents, this translates into solving problems of dispersal. Programs in both the United States and the USSR [Union of Soviet Socialist Republics] devoted years of effort to perfecting these aspects.

Misleading the Public About Biological Warfare

Unfortunately, a recent example provides the sort of grossly uninformed description that is more frequently provided to the general public. Speaking at the Harvard Medical School on June 1, 2005, and trading on his training as a medical doctor as he frequently does, Senator [William H.] Frist claimed that "... a few technicians of middling skill using a few thousand dollars worth of readily available equipment in a small and apparently innocuous setting [could] mount a first-order biological attack. It is even possible to synthesize virulent pathogens from scratch, or to engineer and manufacture prions. .." He repeated that this was "the single greatest threat to our safety and security today." The remarks are a travesty: "... a few *technicians* ... middling skill ... few thousand dollars," leading to a "*first-order*" biological attack, and additionally extending this to "synthesizing virulent pathogens" in the same breath.

The Difficulty in Weaponizing Biological Agents

Most biologicals are not communicable, which means the agent must be delivered to each target individual. Biological agents are susceptible to adverse effects from improper storage, temperatures, humidity or exposure to sunlight, oxygen or other materials. Most have limited shelf life and lose their potency over time. Given the lethal effects of BW agents, they require extremely careful handling.

BW [biological warfare] agents begin in a fluid form, which represents technical challenges to effective dissemination methods. The active agents must be also be reduced to a specific size in the range of 1–5 microns, requiring elaborate and difficult procedures. Converting the materials to dry form offers a number of advantages, but even greater technical prowess and equipment.

The processes are complex and fraught with potential for failure. These are not the kind of tactics favored by terrorists who prefer simple plans, cleverly and flawlessly executed. One does not simply hijack a crop duster and pour BW agents into the tank as a substitute for pesticides.

Global Focus,
"Weapons of Mass Destruction."
http://globalfocus.org.

To bolster his argument, Senator Frist larded his presentation with other gross inaccuracies, claiming that "during the Cold War, the Soviet Union ... stockpiled 5,000 tons *annually* of biowarfare-engineered anthrax resistant to 16 antibiotics." The only source in the world for the tonnage of anthrax stockpiled by the USSR is Dr. Ken Alibek. He has never quoted a figure higher than 200 tons, and he has never claimed that the 200 tons was produced "annually," or in any single year. The USSR's anthrax stockpile consisted of a genetically unmodified classical strain (or strains). The antibiotic resistant strain which was developed by Soviet BW laboratories in the mid- to late-1980s was not resistant to 16 antibiotics, but to half that number, and had not yet reached the point of being stockpiled by the time that the Soviet BW program began to be cut back in 1989. Finally, the 5,000-ton figure is the approximate sum of the annual production capacities of all Soviet-era BW mobilization production facilities that would have initiated production only with the onset of or just prior to a (nuclear) war with the United States. No such quantities of BW agents were ever produced in the USSR. . . .

Clarifying the Facts Regarding Biological Warfare

As best is known from the declassified documents and all the other materials obtained by U.S. military forces in Afghanistan in November and December 2001:

- No al Qaeda capacity for culturing viruses has ever been identified.

- No al Qaeda group has yet been able to obtain a pathogenic strain of anthrax.

- The group operating in Afghanistan in 2000–01 had apparently not yet reached the stage of attempting to culture vaccine strain anthrax. It had been provided with U.S. and UK microbiological journal literature from the 1950s and 1960s. The "methods" sections of those papers would have provided some aid for understanding culturing requirements for anthrax. They would not have assured success in doing it.

- Al Qaeda affiliated groups apparently either have not yet been able to synthesize ricin, or have not yet attempted to do so. . . .

"Bioterrorism" may or may not develop into a serious concern in the future, but it is *not* "one of the most pressing problems that we have on the planet today."

The number of state BW programs has apparently been reduced by one-third or one-fourth in the past 15 years [1990–2005]. The remaining number of countries appears to be stable; no compensating rise in offensive state BW programs has been identified. In addition, the U.S. government—which has almost without exception in past decades been the only country to publicly identify WMD proliferants—appears in its most recent statements to be qualifying the status of states with presumed offensive BW programs. To date, no state is known to have assisted any non-state or terrorist group to obtain biological weapons. . . .

The steps taken by the al Qaeda group in efforts to develop a BW program were more advanced than the United States understood prior to its occupation of Afghanistan in November-December 2001. Nevertheless, publicly available information, including the somewhat ambiguous details that appeared in the March 31, 2005, report of the Commission on the Intelligence Capabilities, indicates that the group failed to obtain and work with pathogens. Should additional information become available regarding the extent to which the al Qaeda BW effort had progressed, that assessment might have to be changed.

Scenarios for national BW exercises that posit various BW agents in advanced states of preparation in the hands of terrorist groups simply disregard the requirements in knowledge and practice that such groups would need in order to work with pathogens. Unfortunately, 10 years of widely broadcast public discussion has provided such groups, at least on a general level, with suggestions as to what paths to follow. If and

when a non-state terrorist group does successfully reach the
stage of working with pathogens, there is every reason to believe that it will involve classical agents, without any molecular
genetic modifications. Preparing a dry powder preparation is
likely to prove difficult, and dispersion to produce mass casualties equally so. Making predictions on the basis of what
competent professionals may find "easy to do" has been a
common error and continues to be so. The utilization of molecular genetic technology by such groups is still further off in
time. No serious military threat assessment imputes to oppo-
nents capabilities that they do not have. There is no justifica-
tion for imputing to real world terrorist groups capabilities in
the biological sciences that they do not possess.

> "Iran has become a country with a rela-
> tively advanced base in biotechnology,
> which has extensive laboratory and re-
> search capability . . . with all of the
> equipment necessary to produce wet
> and dry storable biological weapons."

Iran Has the Capability to Produce Biological Weapons

Anthony H. Cordesman

*Anthony H. Cordesman maintains in the following viewpoint
that Iran presently has the capability to deploy biological weapons and continues its research to develop new types of biological
weapons despite the drawbacks and uncertainties inherent in
their use. He further maintains that Russia has been a key source
in providing Iran with the biotechnology and training for biological warfare production. Cordesman was the former director
of intelligence in the Office of the Secretary of Defense and has
written several books on U.S. security policy.*

Anthony H. Cordesman, *Iranian Weapons of Mass Destruction: Biological Weapons Programs.* Washington, DC: Center for Strategic and International Studies, 2008. Reproduced by permission.

As you read, consider the following questions:

1. What characteristic of biological weapons components makes it impossible to disprove a nation's interest in developing biological weapons, according to the author?

2. In the author's opinion, could Iran's biological weapons be more lethal than fission nuclear weapons?

3. Does Anthony H. Cordesman consider the storage and delivery of weaponized biological agents to be a minor factor of biological warfare?

The world market in biotechnology, food processing, pharmaceutical, and other related equipment has grown so large, has so many dual-use items [for legitimate public health needs such as vaccines and biological warfare], and has such weak controls that it is impossible to know what Iran has purchased and is purchasing, and from whom they are purchasing such items. . . . What is clear is that Iran has become a country with a relatively advanced base in biotechnology, which has extensive laboratory and research capability and steadily improving industrial facilities with dual-use production capabilities with all of the equipment necessary to produce wet and dry storable biological weapons.

Help from the Former Soviet Union

Iran was able to enlist plenty of help in acquiring biotechnology and know-how in the early 1990s. The fall of the Soviet Union—which had been involved in extensive WMD [weapons of mass destruction] research, development, and production throughout the Cold War—left many unemployed Russian scientists looking for new clients. Tehran was able to lure many of these unemployed scientists with knowledge and experience in weaponizing deadly toxins to its program with its abundant reserve of petrodollars.

According to numerous defected former Soviet scientists, several military biologists were recruited by Iran throughout the 1990s. A London *Sunday Times* article from August 1995 reported that "by hiring Russian biological weapons experts, Iran had made a quantum leap forward in its biological weapons program."

In testimony to the Senate Committee on Foreign Relations, John A. Lauder, the director of the Nonproliferation Center at the CIA [Central Intelligence Agency], asserted the following in 2000:

> Iran is seeking expertise and technology from Russia that could advance Tehran's biological warfare effort. Russia has several government-to-government agreements with Iran in a variety of scientific and technical fields.
>
> —Because of the dual-use nature of much of this technology, Tehran can exploit these agreements to procure equipment and expertise that could be diverted to its BW [biological warfare] effort.
>
> —Iran's BW program could make rapid and significant advances if it has unfettered access to BW expertise resident in Russia.

The Acquisition of Biological Warfare Materials

The CIA has continued to provide virtually the same assessments of sales and technology transfer over time. For example, it reported in November 2003 that "even though Iran is part of the BWC [Biological Weapons Convention], Tehran probably maintained an offensive BW program. Iran continued to seek dual-use biotechnical materials, equipment, and expertise. While such materials had legitimate uses, Iran's biological warfare (BW) program also could have benefited from them. It is likely that Iran has capabilities to produce small quantities of BW agents, but has a limited ability to weaponize them."

John R. Bolton, then under secretary for Arms Control and International Security at the U.S. Department of State, provided a more detailed version of such views in testifying to the following to the House International Relations Committee in 2004:

> The U.S. Intelligence Community stated in its recent 721 Report that "Tehran probably maintains an offensive BW program. Iran continued to seek dual-use biotechnical materials, equipment, and expertise. While such materials had legitimate uses, Iran's biological warfare (BW) program also could have benefited from them. It is likely that Iran has capabilities to produce small quantities of BW agents, but has a limited ability to weaponize them."
>
> Because BW programs are easily concealed, I cannot say that the United States can prove beyond a shadow of a doubt that Iran has an offensive BW program. The intelligence I have seen suggests that this is the case, and, as a policy matter therefore, I believe we have to act on that assumption. The risks to international peace and security from such programs are too great to wait for irrefutable proof of illicit activity: Responsible members of the international community should act to head off such threats and demand transparency and accountability from suspected violators while these threats are still emerging. It would be folly indeed to wait for the threat fully to mature before trying to stop it.
>
> Iran is a party to the Biological Weapons Convention (BWC) and the 1925 Protocol for the Prohibition of the Use in War of Asphyxiating, Poisonous or Other Gases, and of Bacteriological Methods of Warfare. Like the CWC [Chemical Weapons Convention], the central obligation of the BWC is simple: no possession, no development, no production, and together with the 1925 Protocol, no use of biological weapons. The overwhelming majority of states parties abide by these obligations. We believe Iran is not abiding by its BWC obligations, however, and we have made this abundantly

clear to the parties of this treaty. It is time for Iran to declare its biological weapons program and make arrangements for its dismantlement.

A Question of Dual-Use Purposes

This creates an ambiguity that cannot be resolved by either US claims or Iranian denials, and this is a problem with most current known and potential proliferators. Many nations now have the biotechnology, the industrial base, and the technical expertise to acquire biological weapons. Not only does most civil technology have "dual use" in building weapons, but the global dissemination of biological equipment has made control by supplier nations extremely difficult. Even when such controls do still apply to original sellers, they have little or no impact on the sellers of used equipment, and a wide range of sensitive equipment is now available for sale to any buyer on the Internet or to any purchasing effort that closely examines the used and surplus equipment sold or disposed of by university and commercial laboratories.

This makes it almost impossible to disprove a nation's interest in biological weapons. Moreover, there is little meaningful distinction between a "defensive" and an "offensive" capability. Nations can claim to be conducting defensive research, acquiring key gear for defensive purposes, and practicing defensive training and maneuvers.

Development and proliferation is made much easier because of the dual-use nature of many of the components necessary for a biological weapons program. According to multiple reports, Chinese, Russian, North Korean, Swiss, Indian, Dutch, German, Italian, Cuban, and Spanish companies—among others—have all provided Iran with biotechnological components and dual-use biological agents that may well have since been incorporated into its biological weapons program.

It is clear, however, that Russia has been a key source of biotechnology for Iran. No US official has ever indicated that

The Potential Coverage and Impact of Various Biological Attacks by Iran

Agent	Downwind Area Kilometers	Number of Casualties Dead	Incapacitated
Rift Valley Fever	1	400	35,000
Tick Borne Encephalitis	1	9,500	35,000
Typhus	5	19,000	85,000
Brucellosis	10	500	125,000
Q Fever	20+	150	125,000
Tularemia	20+	30,000	125,000
Anthrax	20+	95,000	125,000

Note: Assumes 50 kilograms of agent along a two-kilometer line upwind of a population center of 500,000.

TAKEN FROM: George Christopher et al., "Biological Warfare: A Historical Perspective," Journal of the American Medical Association, 278, No. 5, August 6, 1997.

Russia has deliberately supplied Iran with technology or equipment for a biological weapons effort. However, Russia's world-leading expertise in biological weapons makes it a particularly attractive target for Iranians seeking technical information and training on BW agent production processes. This has led to speculation that Iran may have the production technology to make dry storable and aerosol weapons. This would allow it to develop suitable missile warheads, bombs, and covert devices.

These factors make it almost impossible to know how Iran is, or may use, any capabilities it does possess. They also create a situation where if Iran has developed agents for defensive purposes they give it a relatively rapid "breakout" capability to produce offensive agents. Iraq, for example, showed it could rapidly convert a pharmaceutical plant to anthrax production several decades ago, although there is no clear way to determine how lethal its agents would have been.

Possible Scenarios of Bioterrorism Attacks

It is impossible to know what biological agents Iran might actually have weaponized, if only for defensive purposes. Over the years, various sources have cited a range of different possible agents. These included anthrax abotulin toxin, other biotoxins, hoof and mouth disease, Marburg, plague, smallpox, and tularemia. All of these are biological weapons that Iran has long had the technological and manufacturing capability to weaponize, but none has yet been described as having had known tests, as having actually been weaponized, or having been deployed with Iranian forces. Iran also has a sufficiently developed technology base so that it could develop advanced biological agents and weapons, and take advantage of a variety of ways of producing far more lethal weapons than were available during the Cold War. . . .

There are no empirical data to base such estimates upon, and they are little more than "guesstimates." It also is not clear Iran would use a single agent. Most US and FSU [Former Soviet Union] planning for biological warfare during the Cold War called for a mix of biological agents to be used—so-called "biological cocktails." At least some study was given to mixes that would create a focus on the first source of lethality, and lead to the wrong response. Other attacks modeled the use of one biological agent to greatly increase the lethality of another. The modeling of simultaneous and sequential attacks with one agent is uncertain enough, but there are no rules that say a sophisticated terrorist group, or one aided by a state actor, could not use similar "cocktails."

Iran might also attack livestock and agriculture. Annual accidental "attacks" on American agriculture in the form of inadvertent transfers of new pests, diseases, etc. are the rule rather than the exception, and have often had a major impact. Such "attacks" have consisted of importing the wrong pet, diseases brought in the form of a few infected animals or plants, and insects and parasites that have arrived on birds, aircraft, cars, and ships. These have all had major impacts on given crops, and have affected the ecology of whole states, particularly in the southern and western US and Hawaii.

What is clear is that Iran should be able to deploy weapons with at least the lethality that militarized anthrax had reached during the Cold War. . . . It is clear that such biological weapons *could* be as or more lethal than the fission nuclear weapons Iran is likely to be able to acquire within the next half decade. Unlike radiological and chemical weapons, biological weapons can be true weapons of mass destruction. . . .

Iran can also deliver biological attacks by covert or proxy means. A study of possible attack scenarios, developed for defense and response planning by the Department of Homeland Security (DHS), was inadvertently put on the Internet. Among many other cases, it cited the following examples of real-world, near-term possibilities, and ones based on current options that states or non-state actors could actually use.

- Spreading pneumonic plague in the bathrooms of an airport, sports arena, and train station, killing 2,500 and sickening 8,000 worldwide.

- Infecting cattle with foot-and-mouth disease in several places, resulting in hundreds of millions of dollars in losses.

- Exposing an estimated 350,000 people to an anthrax attack by terrorists spraying the biological weapon from a truck driving through five cities over two weeks, according to the report. An estimated 13,200 people could die.

There is a wide range of other agents that Iran might weaponize which differ very sharply in terms of lethality, ease of weaponization, infectiousness, persistence, warning, and treatability. It should also be stressed that lethality is only one measure of the impact of biological weapons, and in most real-world attacks, it may be far less important than the other impacts of such attacks. The immediate and long-term effects of the anthrax scare following 9/11 [2001 terrorist attacks], as well as the Japanese subway attacks, are a prime example that lethality isn't the only measure of success in terms of biological attacks. At the same time, great care should be exercised in assuming that biological attacks necessarily become "weapons of mass media" (WMMs), "weapons of mass panic" (WMPs), or "weapons of mass expenditure" (WMEs). Initial attacks may produce such effects, but governments, media, and publics may well have a more rapid learning curve than some analysts expect. . . .

Future Types of Biological Weapons

While any such analysis is speculative, scientists postulate that the following new types of biological weapons are now deployable or can be manufactured during the coming decade:

- *Binary biological weapons* that use two safe-to-handle elements which can be assembled before use. This could be a virus and helper virus like hepatitis D or a bacterial virulence plasmid like E. coli, plague, anthrax, and dysentery.

- *Designer genes and life forms*, which could include synthetic genes and gene networks, synthetic viruses, and synthetic organisms. These weapons include DNA shuffling, synthetic forms of the flu—which killed more people in 1918 than died in all of World War I and which still kills about 30,000 Americans a year—and synthetic microorganisms.

- *"Gene therapy" weapons* that use transforming viruses or similar DNA vectors carrying Trojan horse genes (retrovirus, adenovirus, poxvirus, HSV-1). Such weapons can produce single individual (somatic cell) or inheritable (germ line) changes. It can also remove immunities and wound healing capabilities.

- *Stealth viruses* can be transforming or conditionally inducible. They exploit the fact that humans normally carry a substantial viral load, and examples are the herpes virus, cytomegalovirus, Epstein-Barr, and SV40 contamination which are normally dormant or limited in infect but can be transformed into far more lethal diseases. They can be introduced over years and then used to blackmail a population.

- *Host-swapping diseases*: Viral parasites normally have narrow host ranges and develop an evolutionary equilibrium with their hosts. Disruption of this equilibrium normally produces no results, but it can be extremely lethal. Natural examples include AIDS, hantavirus, Marburg, and Ebola. Tailoring the disruption for attack purposes can produce weapons that are extremely lethal and for which there is no treatment. A tailored disease like AIDS could combine serious initial lethality with crippling long-term effects lasting decades.

- *Designer diseases* involve using molecular biology to create the disease first and then constructing a pathogen to produce it. It could eliminate immunity, target normally dormant genes, or instruct cells to commit suicide. Apoptosis is programmed cell death, and specific apoptosis can be used to kill any mix of cells.

Storage and delivery of weaponized biological agents is a serious technical challenge that Iran would have to overcome in order to create a serious biological missile arsenal and carry out effective biological attacks. . . .

Doubts about the military effectiveness of biological weapons in tactical combat have resulted in very limited use in recent history, with the exception of the Japanese biological attacks on China during World War II. Biological weapons do present a wide range of drawbacks in addition to the uncertainties regarding their real-world lethality. But despite the uncertainties about performance of biological weapons some states such as Iran continue to research and develop biological agents for the purpose of possible weaponization.

> *"Major infectious diseases known to have potential in biological warfare are endemic in eastern Africa and often cases of emerging disease are reported from the region."*

African Nations Constitute a Unique Biological Weapons Threat

James Thuo Njuguna

In the following viewpoint, James Thuo Njuguna explains that the eastern region of Africa is rife with naturally occurring disease-causing microorganisms, which can be turned into biological weapons against Africans and worldwide. Because Africa is incapable of monitoring these pathogens alone, the author suggests that nations work together to create global disease surveillance and control programs so that the threat posed by biological terrorism can be diminished. Njuguna holds a master's degree in biotechnology and has written several articles about biological and chemical weapons.

James Thuo Njuguna, "Evaluating the Threat of Biological Weapons in Eastern Africa," *African Security Review*, vol. 14, no. 1, 2005. Reproduced by permission of the Institute for Security Studies, www.issafrica.org.

As you read, consider the following questions:

1. According to James Thuo Njuguna, how is the term biological terrorism specifically defined?

2. In the author's opinion, will the future biological warfare threat consist of a large stockpile of weapons?

3. Why does the author believe that all countries in eastern Africa face some level of biological warfare threat?

Deliberate disease is caused through the intentional use of an infectious biological agent or toxin as an act of biological warfare or biological terrorism. The term "biological agent" applies to a diverse group of microorganisms as well as toxins of microorganisms, plants and animals. Biological warfare or biological terrorism is specifically defined as the use of biological agents to deliberately inflict disease and/or death on humans, animals, or plants. When a biological agent is used in the manner described, it is regarded as a biological weapon (BW). Thus crops and livestock as well as human populations are considered possible biological terrorist or biological warfare targets. While some biological agents harm only the exposed population (for example, botulism toxin), infectious agents producing contagious disease (for example, smallpox) could disseminate through susceptible populations unaffected directly by the initial biological terrorist event, as would happen in natural infections.

Biological Agents Have Been Used as Weapons of War

Biological weapons are not new, but the technologies of production and delivery were developed and perfected in the 20th century. For thousands of years biological agents have been available as instruments of warfare and terror, producing fear and harm in vulnerable populations.

Eastern Africa has seen many conflicts since World War II. Freedom wars, inter-state wars, civil wars and ethnic violence are either ongoing or are part of recent history. Economic hardship and inequalities, distrust of government and religious extremism are among the factors that have created a climate in which individuals or groups feel that any action they may take, however heinous, is justified in furthering their cause. This contributes to insecurity in the region and the world at large.

Terror attacks in recent years, such as the bombing of the Oklahoma government building in the US (1995), the US embassy bombings in Kenya and Tanzania (1998), the attacks on the World Trade Center on 11 September 2001, and attacks in Morocco, Indonesia, Russia, Egypt and Spain, have led observers to realise the apparent danger of terrorist threats all over the world. Future terrorist attacks will continue to involve bombs and firearms, but may also involve the use of biological weapons to cause disease.

Biological Agents Are Endemic in Eastern Africa

Major infectious diseases known to have potential in biological warfare are endemic in eastern Africa and often cases of emerging disease are reported from the region. This means that the disease-causing microorganisms occur naturally in the region and are therefore accessible to those with sufficient knowledge to use to deliberately cause disease. This is an adequate reason to presume that eastern Africa, like other regions with similar conditions, faces a potential threat from BW. Outbreaks of Ebola fever (in Uganda and Sudan), Rift Valley fever (in Kenya and Somalia) and yellow fever (in Kenya) have been reported in recent years. The outbreaks of Ebola fever and Rift Valley fever in Uganda and Kenya respectively showed that the region has insufficient resources to deal with such epidemics. A successful deliberate disease attack would probably cripple the public health system. Both lethal and incapacitating agents could have an adverse impact on the civilian health care delivery system in a BW attack scenario. Potential manifestations include terror in the affected population and medical care personnel; an overwhelming number of casualties, placing demands on special medications; a need for personal protection in medical care settings and clinical laboratories; and problems with general handling. . . .

Biomedical research should be managed to ensure that its applications are for peaceful purposes only. The core of future biological warfare threat will probably not consist of a large weapon stockpile, but will probably be the capacity to produce weapons (and their antidotes or phylaxis) on a large scale in a short time or in a crisis. Biotechnology may improve biological warfare capabilities through process and product improvement. This product improvement may involve modifications of pathogens through genetic engineering or through the creation of novel agents and vectors as well as through the development of new equipment for analysis and production. The process of improvement relates to the way agents are manufactured. Optimisation of procedure could lead to production of larger batches within very limited time or the use of small, less conspicuous equipment that is easier to hide in legitimate installations and activities. Genetically modifying existing pathogens may make them more virulent and resistant to drugs and render these agents resistant to environmental stress such as ultraviolet radiation and meteorological conditions after their release to the environment. It is therefore important to have controls in place that will make it less likely for biotechnology to be used to develop or improve biological weapons.

The Likelihood of a Biological Threat Should Be Evaluated

A deliberate disease threat assessment is needed to reduce the uncertainty that currently permeates debate over biological terrorism. Undertaking such a threat assessment is important in the current environment where the public feels insecure and limited resources are available to improve the situation.

An analysis of the threat of use of biological weapons would include identifying which groups or individuals might pose a threat, which agents might be used, how an attack might be carried out, what motivates groups or individuals to use such weapons and which areas would be targeted. Answers to these questions will lead to the development of a number of possible scenarios.

The level of threat is a reflection of the will to use these agents, and not just a technical issue of how to use them. All countries in eastern Africa face some level of threat because of the conflicts and insecurity in the region as well as the easy access to infectious materials.

The impact of the use of biological weapons would be most direct on clinical microbiologists. If a terrorist attack with a biological agent were to occur, medical microbiology laboratories would be instrumental in helping to detect and identify the agent and in alerting authorities. Referral centres should have all necessary resources to support the field laboratories. Although Bacillus anthracis [anthrax] has received a great deal of publicity as a potential biological weapon, other organisms should not be ignored.

Terrorist groups exist to promote religious, ethnic, political (ideological) or economic causes. Acts of biological terrorism could therefore have political, religious, ideological or criminal motives and could conceivably be planned by groups or a single individual or be part of state-sponsored terrorist activities.

The activities leading to the 1998 American embassy bombings in Kenya and Tanzania were well coordinated and planned. This trend has continued with most recent attacks across the world. Various attacks are timed to take place simultaneously and on multiple targets. This indicates that terrorist groups make extensive plans for these activities. It is now known that the suspected perpetrators can be citizens of one or different countries, which demonstrates the capacity of these groups to successfully recruit members and execute plans undetected by law enforcement agencies. This was true of the events of 11 September 2001 in the United States.

When compared to other weapons, the acquisition, storage and transportation of biological weapons could be considerably easier. Competent undergraduate students could readily master viral, bacterial culture methods and simple genetic engineering. It is possible that a group or individuals with appropriate training could produce lethal weapons in adequate amounts and then disseminate them in a manner that would result in thousands of casualties and widespread panic.

Outbreaks of infectious diseases are a common occurrence in eastern Africa and the region suffers from insecurity owing to countless conflicts. This makes the threat of the use of biological weapons in this region something that has to be considered by the relevant government departments. In addition, the distinction between national and global threats is artificial, as infectious agents do not observe the divide. Adequate public health surveillance and response are solutions to preparing for biological warfare events. Only long-term planning and funding can sustain such a global undertaking, which has to be internationally financed and managed. Infectious diseases with no known prophylactic remedies will continue to infect travellers and local people and remain a possible biological weapon.

Disease Control Programs Are Necessary

Infectious diseases can undermine the security of a country whether these diseases are deliberately inflicted by biological warfare or occur naturally. While the Biological and Toxin Weapons Convention (BTWC) prohibits the development and use of biological weapons, the defence against a natural or in-

Biological Agents with the Potential to Be Used for Biological Warfare

More than half of these biological agents are endemic to the Eastern Africa region.

Viruses	
Eastern equine encephalitis virus	Ebola haemorrhagic fever virus
	Junin virus
Sin Nombre virus (hantavirus)	Machupo virus
Lassa fever virus	Rift Valley haemorrhagic fever virus
Marburg virus	
Crimean-congo haemorrhagic fever virus	Tick-borne encephalitis virus
	Venezuelan equine encephalitis virus
Variola major virus (smallpox virus)	
	Yellow fever virus
Western equine encephalitis virus	West Nile haemorrhagic fever virus
Monkeypox virus	Coxiella burnetii (Q fever)
Rickettsiae	Rickettsia rickettsii (spotted fever)
Rickettsia prowazeki (typhus)	
Bacteria	
Brucella sp (brucellosis)	Francisella tularensis tularemia
Burkholderia sp (glanders)	Yersenia pestis (plague)
Bacillus anthracis (anthrax)	
Toxins	
Abrins	Anatoxins
Botulinum toxins	Bungarotoxins
Clostridium toxin	Ciguatoxin
Ricins	Saxitoxin
Shigatoxin	Staphylococcal enterotoxins
Trichothecene toxins	

TAKEN FROM: James Thuo Njuguna, "Evaluating the Threat of Biological Weapons in Eastern Africa," *African Security Review*, vol. 14, no. 1, 2005. Reproduced by permission of the Institute for Security Studies, www.issafrica.org.

tentional epidemic is the same: a robust global public health surveillance system and the ability to respond efficiently and effectively to disease outbreaks. The state has an important role in combating the threat of deliberate disease because it has the moral duty to protect its citizenry.

An effective way of countering the threat of deliberate disease is to establish and maintain disease surveillance and control programmes. Most of the publications on epidemics in eastern Africa indicate that very little disease surveillance is done at present. Where gains were made in control and eradication, they were later lost through neglect of control protocols such as vaccinations and control of livestock movements between endemic and non-endemic areas. There seems to be unanimous agreement among observers that the main reason for the failure of surveillance and control systems is lack of funding. This is blamed on reduced funding for the responsible government organs and agencies owing to shrinking economies. National governments and other interested stakeholders will have to find the required funds, for if infectious diseases are not eradicated or at least maintained at minimum levels, an added threat will be their use as biological weapons, endangering people away from the endemic areas. Observers have expressed the view that disease surveillance should be intensified and coordinated beyond the divide of national boundaries. Surveillance programmes should be part of the public health management systems. The ideal situation requires setting up local and international surveillance/response teams. Teams endowed with the necessary techniques and resources should be put in place so that they can deal with epidemics when they occur. This will ensure that expertise in dealing with these diseases is available uniformly throughout the region. It is also important to register the groups/individuals engaged in these emergencies to minimise chances of hazardous materials being acquired by groups whose intent would be to cause disease outbreaks. Vaccination programmes have to be maintained because failure to do so may lead to a loss of the gains previously achieved in terms of disease control. Besides, for every case of sickness encountered, prevention is cheaper than cure. Some authors encourage joint veterinary and human disease surveillance as a way of cost cutting for zoonotic disease control and such a team can be schooled to monitor biological weapons as well.

Developing countries in general cannot afford to increase spending on health. Any added major spending on health is unlikely to come from national government treasuries. Increased funding for public health systems would have to be sought from wealthier nations and donor agencies. But there is a role for civil society organisations in preventing the use of biological weapons and in ensuring that the damage inflicted by such use is minimised.

Research and Health Systems Should Be Monitored

NGOs [nongovernmental organizations] and professional organizations could monitor the activities of research institutes, industrial concerns and government installations to ensure that research is for peaceful purposes only; monitor the health system to ensure that it has adequate resources to deal with a disease outbreak; and coordinate between countries when crises are encountered, especially during epidemics of diseases that have potential use in BW programmes. The continuous education of emergency department personnel, laboratory technicians, doctors, nurses and public health workers would play a key role in ensuring that there is a high level of preparedness to detect and manage epidemics. Workshops/ seminars and refresher courses on case management, drug use and diagnosis should be regularly undertaken or be made part of continuing education.

Information gaps exist for some of the important infectious diseases endemic in the region and these can be bridged by information generated through new research. New research could lead to new products that would aid in the management of these infectious diseases. These information gaps exist on diseases such as brucellosis, plague, anthrax, rickettsial diseases and haemorrhagic fevers, endemic to the eastern African region. Studies centred on epidemiology and biology aspects of these infectious agents would bridge the information gap and hence increase knowledge of these diseases in the region.

Researchers could generate specific materials and information that can be used as tools for training health practitioners and as reference materials for the diseases. The use, for example, of molecular probes would shed some new light on the epidemiology of these diseases and validate their use (probes) for general diagnosis, hence creating new tools for disease surveillance. Research should also be directed towards the development of vaccines against the agents of haemorrhagic fevers as the existing vaccine is only for yellow fever.

Global Cooperation Should Be Strengthened

It is vital that the international community should ensure that there is compliance with the BTWC, which prohibits the hostile use of disease against humans, animals, or plants. A number of researchers and governments have favoured linking the BTWC to specific measures for fighting infectious diseases and the transfer of relevant technology and expertise to achieve this end. For example, a measure that became known as the Vaccines for Peace Programme was proposed to counteract the threat of both deliberate and natural disease. A second proposal was made to establish a global disease surveillance programme. If institutionalised, these measures may have had the capacity to limit the threat posed by deliberate disease. Some international institutions, such as the Office International des Epizooties (OIE), the UN Food and Agriculture Organization

(FAO) and WHO [World Health Organization], are seen as appropriate bodies for implementing such programmes.

While the BTWC is, in general, designed to prevent the transfer of BW materials and technology, Article X does encourage "the fullest possible exchange of equipment, materials and scientific and technological information for the use of bacteriological (biological) agents and toxins for peaceful purposes." The spirit of this article underlines the need for state parties to cooperate in defeating disease, by developing cures, vaccines, and surveillance tools. Not only is this of benefit to developing states, but it is the best guarantee of diminishing the threat posed by deliberate disease.

In 2004 the states parties to the BTWC held expert and political meetings to consider "enhancing international capabilities for responding to, investigating and mitigating the effects of cases of alleged use of biological or toxin weapons or suspicious outbreaks of disease; and strengthening and broadening national and international institutional efforts and existing mechanisms for the surveillance, detection, diagnosis and combating of infectious diseases affecting humans, animals and plants." A global response to the containment of infectious diseases through the provision of vaccine and surveillance tools is necessary to ensure that a country which reports a rare disease occurrence will not just be reporting out of fear of retribution for failing to make such a report, but because they would receive support to contain the outbreak.

The recent outbreaks of SARS [severe acute respiratory syndrome] and the continuing AIDS epidemic have demonstrated critical weaknesses in global public health infrastructure in the face of a threat from a novel pathogen. The international community must continue to learn from the experience of natural outbreaks to improve early detection and effective response to emerging disease on a global basis. Minimising the impact of disease, of natural or deliberate origin, will save countless lives as well as deter future bioterrorist acts.

Periodical Bibliography

The following articles have been selected to supplement the diverse views presented in this chapter.

Fred Burton and Scott Stewart — "Placing the Terrorist Threat to the Food Supply in Perspective," *Right Side News*, April 22, 2008.

Sara A. Carter — "Al Qaeda Eyes Bio Attack from Mexico," *Washington Times*, June 3, 2009.

Elaine M. Grossman — "Drug Safety Watchdog Sees al-Qaeda Risk to U.S. Food, Drug Imports," *Global Security Newswire*, January 29, 2009.

Gardiner Harris — "U.S. Food Safety No Longer Improving, CDC Says," *New York Times*, April 10, 2009.

Sarah Hills — "Food Terrorism Tops 2009 Safety Scare List," January 5, 2009. www.FoodNavigator-USA.com.

International Crisis Group — "North Korea's Chemical and Biological Weapons Programs," June 18, 2009.

Alex Kingsbury — "Where the Terrorism Threat from al Qaeda Is Headed," *U.S. News & World Report*, January 12, 2009.

Alan Pearson — "The Expanding Range of Biowarfare Threats," *Bulletin of the Atomic Scientists*, March 2008.

Jason Sigger — "Chemical, Biological Arms: Iran's *Other* WMDs," *Wired*, October 29, 2008. www.wired.com.

Eileen Sullivan — "Homeland Security's 5-Year Threat Picture," *Washington Times*, December 25, 2008.

CHAPTER 3

How Should the United States Prepare for Biological Warfare?

Chapter Preface

Even after the terrorist attacks in 2001 and all the recent dire warnings of possible terrorist attacks to come, experts claim that most Americans are not prepared for a major national emergency. In fact, studies have shown that less than one-third of all Americans have taken steps to prepare for an emergency, and a June 2007 Harris poll found that only 14 percent of respondents said they are "very prepared." Dennis O'Leary, former president of the Joint Commission on Accreditation of Healthcare Organizations, termed the nation's attitude "comfortable complacency." Preparedness and emergency-response authorities are concerned about such public complacency and worry that citizens rely too heavily on state and federal governments to provide for them should the need arise. Thomas H. Kean, the 9/11 Commission chairman, put it this way: "The weakest part of our homeland security is the citizen."

Part of the problem is that many people do not know what to prepare for and feel overwhelmed by all the possibilities. An earthquake? A flu pandemic? A bioterrorist attack? Such uncertainty often leads to a wait-and-see attitude, which in itself can be a prescription for disaster, according to authorities. Instead, mental health specialists advise citizens not to concentrate on factors beyond their control—such as how or when a calamity will strike—but on those factors over which they do have control. Preparing a family emergency plan, which should include how to get information and communicate with one another; developing an evacuation plan; putting together a supplies kit—all of these proactive steps can create a sense of empowerment and resilience in citizens, and by extension, in communities. Education is also important. For example, understanding the difference between "quarantine," which applies to persons who have been exposed to a contagious disease but who may or may not become ill, and "isolation," which applies to those who are known to be ill with a contagious disease, could prove valuable during a biological warfare attack. Furthermore, a 2008 report cosponsored by the Robert Wood Johnson Foundation titled *Ready or Not? Protecting the Public's Health from Diseases, Disasters, and Bioterrorism* states that because children under the age of eighteen represent one-quarter of the U.S. population, emergency preparedness should be part of schools' curriculum, and staff and students should have emergency response plans in place and conduct practice drills.

Many experts agree that during a crisis, individuals, families, and communities play an important role, and those who are prepared and resilient will fare better than those who are not. A culture of preparedness must replace the culture of complacency, they assert. John D. Solomon summed it up in his May 2008 article, "It's an Emergency. We're Not Prepared." for the *Washington Post*: "Being prepared may be the most significant contribution many citizens can make to their nation's security." The authors in this chapter examine various measures that the U.S. government should take to prepare for biological warfare.

> *"It is plain to see that our own scores of laboratories that study biological weapons agents represent the easiest avenue by which a would-be bioterrorist could obtain the materials and knowledge necessary to commit crime in the United States."*

The Expansion of Biodefense Research Laboratories Needs Increased Oversight

Edward Hammond

In the following viewpoint, Edward Hammond contends that the large expansion of laboratories handling biological weapons agents in the United States poses significant safety and security risks such as researchers acquiring infectious diseases, unauthorized persons handling biological weapons agents, and irregular accounting and documentation practices. He maintains that without increased oversight, these research centers represent easy targets from which terrorists can gain access to technical knowledge and dangerous pathogens to commit biological warfare.

Edward Hammond, "Written Testimony of Edward Hammond, Submitted to the Subcommittee on Oversight and Investigations for the Hearing: *Germs, Viruses, and Secrets: The Silent Proliferation of Bio-Laboratories in the United States*," U.S. House of Representatives, Committee on Energy and Commerce, October 4, 2007. Reproduced by permission of the author.

Hammond, an American policy researcher, has focused his work on biotechnology-related policy.

As you read, consider the following questions:

1. In the author's opinion, should some of the planned biological weapons research centers be appropriated for other uses?

2. Does the public have a right to know details about accidents that occur in biodefense research facilities, according to Edward Hammond?

3. According to the author, has the Centers for Disease Control and Prevention (CDC) discovered safety and security problems during cause inspections of biodefense research facilities?

As evidenced by the offensive biological weapons activities of the Soviet Union in its waning years as well as those of Iraq prior to the first Gulf War, the United States needs a biological defense program. In addition, the rate of discovery in biotechnology fields including genetic engineering and synthetic biology and the proliferation of associated knowledge merit assessment of a biodefense program, strictly and always in ways permitted by the Biological and Toxin Weapons Convention. For those reasons and following the events of 2001 [9/11 terrorist attacks and domestic anthrax attacks], an expansion of the US biodefense program was merited and this expansion would logically include new and/or upgraded laboratory facilities commensurate with an increased effort.

In the past 6 years [2001–2007], however, lab expansion under the [George W.] Bush administration has gone far beyond what is prudent and necessary, and without an adequate regulatory framework. According to the most recent statements by the Centers for Disease Control [CDC], there are now approximately 400 facilities and 15,000 people in the United States handling biological weapons agents. Many of these facilities are new and are staffed by scientists and others with little to no prior experience with biological weapons agents and the safety and security measures they require. In addition they are frequently on college campuses and other locations where rule-based systems of strict accountability are absent and, in fact, alien to institutional culture. It is plain to see that our own scores of laboratories that study biological weapons agents represent the easiest avenue by which a would-be bioterrorist could obtain the materials and knowledge necessary to commit crime in the United States.

Thus, a reduction in the number of facilities and persons handling biological weapons agents is a highly desirable step for both safety and security. This could include cancellation or conversion of some planned and under-construction facilities and rerouting of some appropriations toward basic research and public health, to help address the health problems that Americans most frequently face, which are not at all typically caused by biological weapons agents.

Inadequate Transparency Undermines Democracy and Safety

Research with biological weapons agents must be transparent and publicly accountable. A culture of transparency does not presently exist. Laboratories would be more likely to conduct research in a prudent and safe manner with the public able to look over their shoulder. Access to records such as research protocols, safety minutes, and accident reports will help ensure that studies are conducted with public safety and security in mind and, most importantly, reassure other countries of the peaceful intent and activities of the US biodefense program. . . .

Accidents and other safety and security problems have resulted from expansion of research involving biological weapons agents. These include laboratory-acquired infections with biological weapons agents, unauthorized persons handling biological weapons agents, failure to account for stocks of biological weapons agents, and other problems.

It should be initially noted that the public's right to know about lab accidents is largely ignored, and information on them is very difficult to acquire. The Centers for Disease Control refuses all FOIA [Freedom of Information Act] requests for such information and the NIH [National Institutes of Health] Office of Biotechnology Activities has not produced its data, although there is good reason to question its reliability, if NIH data exist. In general, it is only possible for the public to acquire information about laboratory mishaps in the limited number of cases where labs are a) subject to open records rules sufficiently powerful to enable access to accident documentation, and b) have policies to record incidents. There is mounting evidence that at many facilities there have been *de facto* policies not to record accidents, including accidents with biological weapons agents.

Texas A&M University (TAMU) is a Department of Homeland Security [DHS] National Center of Excellence in the study of biological weapons agents, and is the lead institution in the DHS National Center for Foreign Animal and Zoonotic Disease Defense. Through the Texas Public Information Act, and significant pressure on TAMU officials, it was established that in 2006 and 2007 the university committed numerous violations of the Bioterrorism Act of 2002 (implemented by the Select Agent Rule). The most serious of these included an unreported lab-acquired infection with *Brucella sp.* and multiple unreported exposures to Q fever (*Coxiella burnetii*). CDC investigations prompted by Sunshine Project [an international nongovernmental organization dedicated to preventing abuse of biotechnology until the project's suspension on February 1, 2008] news releases documented additional serious violations that include more unreported lab exposures and irregularities in accounting for biological weapons agents and, importantly, that TAMU repeatedly permitted access to and handling of biological weapons agents by persons lacking federal permission to do so. In fact, the brucellosis victim was one such person.

Accidents at University
Research Laboratories

In addition to the incidents at Texas A&M, analysis of biosafety committee minutes show other accidents involving select agents [biological agents and toxins that pose a severe threat to human health] and/or BSL-3 labs:

At the University of Wisconsin at Madison in 2005 and 2006, researchers handled genetic copies of the entire Ebola virus (called "full length cDNAs") at BSL [biosafety level]-3, despite the fact that the NIH guidelines require handling at BSL-4 because the genetic constructs had not been rendered irreversibly incapable of producing live virus. The University of Wisconsin at Madison Institutional Biosafety Committee reviewed and approved this research despite federal guidelines to the contrary. The problem was not detected by NIH. In fact, NIH funded the research.

There is evidence that a situation similar to Wisconsin's exists or existed at Tulane University in New Orleans, Louisiana, which also does not have appropriate labs for such research. Tulane officials refused a half dozen requests to clarify the research, again with Ebola cDNAs as well as constructs for Lassa fever virus, another BSL-4 hemorrhagic fever agent.

At the University of Texas at Austin in April 2006, human error and equipment (centrifuge) malfunction combined in an incident in a BSL-3 lab handling potentially very dangerous genetically-engineered crosses between H5N1 "bird flu" and typical (H3N2) human influenza. The researcher was placed on drugs, the lab shut down and decontaminated. The university did not report the incident to the federal government and has since produced conflicting accounts of what exactly happened.

In mid-2003, a University of New Mexico (UNM) researcher was jabbed with an anthrax-laden needle. The following year, another UNM researcher experienced a needle stick with an unidentified (redacted) pathogenic agent that had been genetically engineered.

At the Medical University of Ohio in late 2004, a researcher was infected with Valley Fever (*Coccidioides immitis*), a BSL-3 biological weapons agent. The following summer (2005), a serious lab accident occurred that resulted in exposure of one or more workers to an aerosol of the same agent.

In mid-2005, a lab worker at the University of Chicago punctured his or her skin with an infected instrument bearing a BSL-3 biological weapons agent. It was likely a needle contaminated with either anthrax or plague bacteria.

In October and November of 2005, the University of California [UC] at Berkeley received dozens of samples of what it thought was a relatively harmless organism. In fact, the samples contained Rocky Mountain Spotted Fever bacteria, classified as a BSL-3 bioweapons agent because of its potential for transmission by aerosol. As a result, the samples were handled without adequate safety precautions until the mistake was discovered. Unlike nearby Children's Hospital & Research Center Oakland, which previously experienced a widely reported anthrax bacteria mix-up, UC Berkeley never told the community.

Disregard for Safety Protocols

In addition to lab-acquired infections and exposures, other types of dangerous problems have occurred, such as unauthorized research, equipment malfunction, and disregard for safety protocols:

In February 2005 at the University of Iowa, researchers performed genetic engineering experiments with tularemia bacteria without permission. They included mixing genes from tularemia species and introducing antibiotic resistance.

Laboratory Biosafety Level (BSL) Criteria

BSL	Agents	Practices
1	Not known to consistently cause diseases in healthy adults	Standard Microbiological Practices
2	• Agents associated with human disease • Routes of transmission include percutaneous injury, ingestion, mucous membrane exposure	BSL-1 practice plus: • Limited access • Biohazard warning signs • "Sharps" precautions • Biosafety manual defining any needed waste decontamination or medical surveillance policies
3	• Indigenous or exotic agents with potential for aerosol transmission • Disease may have serious or lethal consequences	BSL-2 practice plus: • Controlled access • Decontamination of all waste • Decontamination of laboratory clothing before laundering • Baseline serum
4	• Dangerous/exotic agents which pose high risk of life-threatening disease • Aerosol-transmitted laboratory infections have occurred; or related agents with unknown risk of transmission	BSL-3 practice plus: • Clothing change before entering • Shower on exit • All material decontaminated on exit from facility

TAKEN FROM: U.S. Department of Health and Human Services, *Biosafety in Microbiological and Biomedical Laboratories*, 5th Edition, 2007.

In September 2004 at the University of Illinois at Chicago, lab workers at a BSL-3 facility propped open doors of the lab and its anteroom, a major violation of safety procedures. An alarm that should have sounded did not.

In March 2005 at the University of North Carolina at Chapel Hill, lab workers were exposed to tuberculosis when the BSL-3 lab's exhaust fan failed. Due to deficiencies in the lab, a blower continued to operate, pushing disease-laden air out of a safety cabinet and into the room. An alarm, which would have warned of the problem, had been turned off. The lab had been inspected and approved by the US Army one month earlier.

In December 2005 at the Albert Einstein College of Medicine at Yeshiva University in New York City, three lab workers were exposed (seroconverted) to the tuberculosis bacterium following experiments in a BSL-3 lab. The experiments involved a Madison Aerosol Chamber, the same device used in the February 2006 experiments that resulted in the Texas A&M brucella case.

In mid-2004, a steam valve from the biological waste treatment tanks failed at Building 41A on the NIH Campus in Bethesda, Maryland. The building houses BSL-3 and BSL-4 labs. Major damage was caused, and the building was closed for repairs.

In April 2007, a centrifuge problem exposed several lab workers at the University of Texas Health Science Center in Houston to anthrax.

Also in April 2007, three lab workers entered a laboratory studying tularemia at the University of Texas at San Antonio to repair faulty air filters. The workers did not wear respiratory protection and handled the filter equipment without gloves.

It is very important to note that these and other examples of lab accidents are drawn from biosafety committee meeting minutes of institutions that actually record such incidents in records that are (at least nominally) available to the public. Often, this is not the case, such as that of Texas A&M, which only released accident information under extreme pressure.

Thus, the sample of institutions named above is (mostly) skewed toward those that have been more open about their accidents than others. . . .

Inadequate Inspection Procedures

It is apparent that CDC inspections have not identified significant problems at laboratories handling biological weapons agents. This is clearest at Texas A&M University, where the Texas Public Information Act has caused release of a large amount of documentation from TAMU's biosafety and biosecurity program and CDC's inspections. CDC's cause inspections of Texas A&M in April and July of this year [2007] revealed numerous problems that existed but were not detected during CDC's previous routine inspections.

Routine CDC inspection did not detect the fact that TAMU had permitted unauthorized persons to handle biological weapons agents, even though the incident in which an unauthorized researcher contracted brucellosis occurred before CDC's 2006 inspection at TAMU. Other problems CDC inspectors failed to discover include a researcher who stuck him or herself with a *Brucella*-laden needle in 2004, multiple exposures to Q fever in 2006, and inadequate ventilation of [a] major piece of lab equipment (an aerosol chamber) used with biological weapons agents. A number of additional missed violations are documented in the reports of the CDC cause inspections following the cease and desist orders issued to TAMU. . . .

Inadequate Oversight of Nucleic Acids

A major flaw in the existing Select Agent Rule is that, as interpreted by the CDC, it fails to adequately cover nucleic acids (DNA, RNA) that can be use to produce select agents.

For many viruses, including several select agent viruses such as 1918 influenza, H5N1 avian influenza, and Ebola viruses, it is possible to produce [a] fully infectious virus from nucleic acids comprising the virus genome. This can be accomplished in short periods of time, in some cases in less than two days and without any specialized equipment that would not be typically present in a university or private sector virology lab.

The Select Agent Rule contains language covering nucleic acids that can produce select agents (*"Nucleic acids that can produce infectious forms of any of the select agent viruses. . ."* are classified as select agents). But contrary to the language of the rule, CDC has interpreted it to cover only those nucleic acids that are, in effect, full-fledged disease agents and which can cause infection through injection, inhalation, or exposure without any further manipulation.

These flaws effectively enable unregulated possession of several select agent viruses. The threat posed by this flaw is increasing in direct proportion to the rapid development of DNA synthesis technology and the DNA synthesis industry as well as the related field of synthetic biology, which is dramatically decreasing the cost, time, and difficulty of producing a nucleic acid that can be used to produce a select agent.

This is not a theoretical concern. It is currently happening in US labs.

Advances in DNA sequencing technology and in the related field of synthetic biology, where scientists construct living systems from nucleic acid building blocks, are heightening the chances that these kinds of biotechnology could be used for biological weapons purposes. While members of the DNA synthesis industry and some synthetic biologists have indicated their concern and even openness to discuss regulation, for instance through a "Select DNA (RNA) Rule," there does not appear to have been any practical movement forward by CDC on this issue, and full length nucleic acids, as well as those encoding major portions of select agents, remain outside the Select Agent Rule as interpreted by the CDC.

"The NIH [National Institutes of Health] is committed to the highest quality in the design and construction of these facilities, the rigorous training of the personnel that operate them, and the safe conduct of the research undertaken within them."

The Expansion of Biodefense Research Laboratories Has Sufficient Oversight for Safety

Hugh Auchincloss

In the following viewpoint, Hugh Auchincloss maintains that the construction of additional U.S. biodefense research centers is absolutely necessary to protect the nation from emerging disease threats—whether from biological war or acts of nature. He further maintains that the National Institutes of Health (NIH) has participated in many public forums regarding the safety of the new facilities and supports vigorous biosafety training and monitoring. Auchincloss, a physician, is the deputy director of the National Institute of Allergy and Infectious Diseases (NIAID), which is a component of the National Institutes of Health.

Hugh Auchincloss, "Statement Given to the Subcommittee on Oversight and Investigations of the House Committee on Energy and Commerce for the Hearing: *Germs, Viruses, and Secrets: The Silent Proliferation of Bio-Laboratories in the United States*," U.S. House of Representatives, 110th Congress, 1st session, October 4, 2007, pp. 75–78.

As you read, consider the following questions:

1. Has Congress supported funding for research involving pathogens and contagious microbial agents, according to the author?

2. According to Hugh Auchincloss, what type of agents do Biosafety Level 4 (BSL-4) laboratory researchers study?

3. According to the author, is all biodefense research conducted only by government agencies, such as the Department of Defense?

The anthrax attacks in 2001 were a sobering reminder that the threat of deliberately released microbes can be used as a form of terrorism. Moreover, naturally occurring microbial outbreaks pose a serious threat to domestic and global health. The experience with SARS [severe acute respiratory syndrome] in 2003 and the ongoing outbreaks of H5N1 avian influenza and extensively drug-resistant tuberculosis have reminded us that defense against naturally emerging microbes must be a top national priority. Congress has recognized the urgency of improving our defenses against emerging public health threats and has supported funding for such research. Within the broad federal effort against emerging threats to public health, the role of the NIH [National Institutes of Health] is to conduct and support basic and applied research that will lead to new vaccines, drugs, and diagnostic tools.

A Shortage of Research Laboratories

In February 2002, the NIH embarked on a systematic planning process for its biodefense research program. It first convened the Blue Ribbon Panel on Bioterrorism and Its Implications for Biomedical Research, made up of distinguished scientists representing academia, private industry, and government. Based on the panel's advice and extensive discussions with other federal agencies, the NIH developed three key documents to guide its biodefense research program: the NI-AID [National Institute of Allergy and Infectious Disease] Strategic Plan for Biodefense Research, the NIAID Research Agenda for Category A Agents, and the NIAID Research Agenda for Category B and C Agents.

As a result of the strategic planning process, a clear consensus emerged that meeting the goals of the biodefense Research Agendas would require additional research infrastructure, especially research laboratories built to modern Biosafety Level 3 (BSL-3) and Biosafety Level 4 (BSL-4) standards. BSL-3 laboratories are used to study contagious agents that can be transmitted through the air and cause potentially lethal infection. BSL-4 laboratories are used to study agents that pose a high risk of life-threatening disease for which no vaccine or therapy is available; they incorporate all BSL-3 features and occupy safe, isolated zones within a larger building.

There has been considerable discussion of how best to assess the extent of high-containment facilities that would be required in the United States in the public, academic and private sectors and for what purposes these varied facilities are used. Published estimates range from as few as 200 to as many as 1400 BSL-3 laboratories. (Many institutions maintain multiple facilities.) The explanation for this wide discrepancy is that an assessment of laboratory capacity depends on the definitions and sources of information used. Estimates at the high end, for example, include the many hospitals that maintain small areas that meet BSL-3 standards that can be used for testing clinical samples that might contain infectious agents. These are not "research laboratories." Some hospitals, pharmaceutical companies, biotechnology firms, private reference laboratories, and state public health laboratories also have facilities that meet BSL-3 standards, but these are not generally available for NIH-sponsored research. Finally, many BSL-3 facilities constructed before the mid-1990s cannot support research on select agents and on associated animal models. In

2002, NIAID determined that very little usable BSL-3 or BSL-4 research space was actually available for its academic scientists in the extramural research program.

Legislation for Funding Biodefense Facilities

The Blue Ribbon Panel of 2002 noted the shortage of BSL-3 and BSL-4 laboratory space as a significant rate-limiting obstacle in accomplishing the objectives of the NIAID Biodefense Research Agendas. In response, NIAID estimated the new BSL-3 and BSL-4 facilities that would be required to accomplish the Research Agenda. Congress also recognized the critical need for new BSL-3/4 laboratories and responded quickly to supply the necessary resources to fulfill this need. In 2002, the Department of Defense and Emergency Supplemental Appropriations for Recovery from and Response to Terrorist Attacks on the Unites States Act, Public Law (P.L.) 107–117, appropriated $70 million for the construction and renovation of NIH intramural biocontainment facilities. The Consolidated Appropriations Act of 2003, P.L. 108–7, provided $372.6 million to NIAID for construction of extramural biocontainment facilities and $291 million for construction of additional intramural biocontainment facilities. Further, the Project BioShield Act of 2004 (P.L. 108–276), amended the Public Health Service Act to provide ongoing authority to NIAID to award grants and contracts for construction of research facilities. An additional $150 million was appropriated for NIAID in the 2005 Consolidated Appropriations Act (P.L. 108–447) for extramural facilities construction grants.

The NIH is now implementing a construction program that will complete 14 new BSL-3 facilities and 4 new BSL-4 facilities within the next several years. During this process, the NIH or its funded institutions have participated in literally hundreds of public forums on the nature and safety of the new facilities, and have submitted reports to Congress annually, along with periodic updates on our strategic plans. In addition, NIH leadership has discussed the infrastructure expansion with Congress on many occasions. And because NIH does not fund or conduct classified research, the title and substance of every research project funded by the NIH is publicly available.

Another important aspect of the biodefense research infrastructure is a network of ten NIH-funded Regional Centers of Excellence for Biodefense and Emerging Infectious Diseases Research (RCEs). Created in 2003, these multidisciplinary academic research programs are located at institutions across the country and provide the scientific expertise for a wide-ranging biodefense research program directed against deliberate and naturally-occurring threats that will be pursued in the new facilities.

High Level of Safety and Training

The NIH is committed to helping ensure that all biodefense research facilities provide maximum protection for public health. The NIH is committed to the highest quality in the design and construction of these facilities, the rigorous training of the personnel that operate them, and the safe conduct of the research undertaken within them.

To ensure that the new laboratories are designed and constructed to the highest standards, the NIAID works closely with each grantee institution. Highly experienced NIAID staff architects and engineers, with extensive experience in design of biocontainment facilities, are assisted by a Construction Quality Management group of contracted consultants with additional expertise. Together, these teams make certain that the finished projects will meet the regulations of HHS's [Department of Health and Human Services'] Centers for Disease Control and Prevention (CDC) and the Department of Agriculture's Animal and Plant Health Inspection Service (USDA/APHIS) for facilities that conduct research on select agents.

The NIH also supports a vigorous biosafety and biocontainment training effort that has expanded substantially over the past five years. The National Biosafety and Biocontainment Training Program (NBBTP) is a partnership between the NIAID and the NIH Division of Occupational Health and Safety (DOHS), managed by a not-for-profit education and research foundation. The mission of this program is to prepare biosafety and biocontainment professionals of the highest caliber. The program offers two-year post-baccalaureate and post-doctoral fellowships at NIH's campus in Bethesda, Maryland, with both academic and hands-on training. The NBBTP has also provided training for containment laboratory operation and maintenance personnel across the country. In addition to this program, NIAID funds 28 Institutional Training Grants in Biodefense, and the RCEs conduct extensive training in biosafety and biocontainment. At the RCE at Emory University in Atlanta, for example, trainees from across the country regularly participate in BSL-3 and BSL-4 training in mock laboratories, constructed specifically for training purposes.

When these new facilities are ready for operation, NIH is committed to ensuring that the research conducted within them is performed safely. The most widely used guidance on the safe conduct of this research is the *Biosafety in Microbiological and Biomedical Laboratories Manual* (BMBL), which was first produced jointly in 1984 by the NIH and CDC and which is now in its fifth edition and available online.

Involvement of Many Agencies for Oversight

Monitoring adherence to good laboratory practices is a complex process because multiple agencies are involved. Much of the research in BSL-3 and BSL-4 facilities involves pathogens that have been designated as select agents. CDC and APHIS have the responsibility for regulating the possession, use, and transfer of select agents. For research that involves recombi-

Oversight of Select Agents by the Centers for Disease Control and Prevention

Even in the best of laboratories, which follow all bio-safety guidelines, accidents like a broken test tube or a needle stick can still occur, and we can expect that we will continue to receive reports of possible losses and releases of select agents. However, we believe we should always strive to eliminate all incidents. Appropriately contained and managed laboratories have multiple systems in place to ensure biosafety and have robust occupational health services in place to quickly mitigate the effect of any laboratory incident. We also believe that the security requirements put in place by the select agent regulations will continue to mitigate the possibility of a theft of a select agent.

Richard E. Besser,
Testimony Before the Subcommittee on Oversight
and Investigations, Committee on Energy and Commerce,
U.S. House of Representatives, October 4, 2007.

nant [genetically engineered] DNA, the select agent regulations incorporate the NIH Guidelines for Research Involving Recombinant DNA Molecules (Recombinant DNA Guidelines) as a consideration in the entity's development of its biosafety plan. The NIH Office of Biotechnology Activities (OBA), with advice and guidance from the NIH Recombinant DNA Advisory Committee (RAC), is responsible for implementation of the Recombinant DNA Guidelines, which outlines biosafety and containment, standards for research involving recombinant DNA. Also, the select agent regulations require that restricted experiments such as the deliberate transfer of a drug-resistant trait to a select agent must be approved by CDC or APHIS prior to initiation. However, some research conducted in BSL-3 facilities involves neither select agents nor recombinant DNA.

Local institutional bodies play a very important role in oversight of many aspects of biomedical research. For example, oversight to protect human subjects in clinical studies is provided by local Institutional Review Boards (IRBs), and in the case of animal research, oversight to ensure humane treatment is provided by the Institutional Animal Care and Use Committees (IACUCs). The NIH Guidelines mandate that Institutional Biosafety Committees (IBCs) oversee recombinant DNA research, but many institutions have gradually broadened IBC responsibilities to include oversight of research involving all pathogens studied at BSL-3 and BSL-4 levels. At this time there is no federal body that sets national standards or policies for this function of local IBCs, and adherence to BMBL guidelines for BSL-3 and BSL-4 research is voluntary; however, the select agents regulations require regulated entities to comply with the BMBL guidelines or equivalent standards.

The NIH is deeply concerned about recent reports of accidents occurring in BSL-3 facilities. When these events involve recombinant DNA, they are reported to the OBA, and a root cause analysis is done so that NIH can assess the adequacy of the institution's response and work with the institution to put mechanisms in place to mitigate the chance of a reoccurrence. To enhance all of the functions of the IBCs, the NIH has worked intensively with the IBC community. These efforts have included an extensive program of outreach and education, involving frequent daylong training sessions, exhibits at major scientific conferences, policy guidances, educational resources for institutions to use in local training, and other means. Furthermore, each of the institutions receiving one of the new facilities construction grants from NIAID has an IBC appropriately registered with NIH and each has willingly accepted responsibility for adhering to BMBL standards.

The NIH is examining ways to strengthen local and federal oversight of facilities that conduct NIH-funded research. The issues associated with oversight of research in BSL-3 and BSL-4 facilities transcend the NIH, or even the HHS. Biodefense research involving BSL-3 and BSL-4 facilities is conducted by many government agencies, including the Department of Defense (DoD), the Department of Homeland Security (DHS), and the USDA, as well as by universities and biotechnology companies. As I noted earlier, BSL-3 facilities exist in hospitals for routine handling of clinical samples. It is important to devise a framework that improves oversight, training, and reporting to enhance safety without causing unintended negative consequences for either patient care or the biodefense research program. For that reason, HHS, USDA, DHS, and DoD have already agreed to establish a Trans-Federal Task Force to undertake, in consultation with other relevant agencies, an intensive analysis of the current biosafety framework and to develop a set of recommendations for improvement. Given the critical importance of biosafety to protecting public health and the concerns that the high containment facilities engender among local communities, active participation in this process from the public at large will be essential.

Substantial Achievements in Biodefense

Support for infrastructure for biodefense research is essential if we are to fulfill our biodefense research agenda and protect the nation from disease threats, be they deliberate or acts of nature. We have already made substantial progress with the facilities now available. For example, NIH-funded scientists have developed a safer second-generation smallpox vaccine called ACAM2000 and a very promising new smallpox drug named ST-246. Investigators have developed and tested a new anthrax vaccine called rPA and have achieved promising results with antibodies capable of neutralizing anthrax toxins. They have developed first- and second-generation vaccines against Ebola virus, and investigated a promising Ebola therapy based on RNA interference. These and many other advances required the use of containment facilities of the type that are now under construction. Progress should occur more rapidly as the new facilities become available.

NIH-funded biodefense researchers are acutely aware of the threat posed by the pathogens they study. These experts understand the need to handle them with utmost care, the need for rigorous training and state-of-the-art equipment, and the need to scrupulously follow all required procedures. Their awareness also includes a deep understanding that the nation's biosecurity depends on their work, which is the conduct of research that will lead to new tools essential to meet emerging and re-emerging threats to public health.

> "We must do everything we can to make sure that biological agents and toxins that could present a serious threat to public health are kept safe and secure in containment laboratories and out of the hands of terrorists."

Proposed Legislation Will Significantly Improve the Select Agent Program

Richard Burr

In the following viewpoint, Republican senator Richard Burr from North Carolina maintains that the United States should give bioterrorism a higher priority and, to that end, enhance the nation's biosecurity programs. To accomplish that goal, Burr supports legislation (Senate Bill 485) that would increase oversight of all U.S. biodefense research laboratories and update the Select Agent Program so that the latest scientific advances of biological weapons agents would be considered.

As you read, consider the following questions:

1. For what purpose was the Select Agent Program created, according to Richard Burr?

Richard Burr, "Statement to the U.S. Senate on Introduced Bills and Joint Resolutions," *Congressional Record*, February 26, 2009.

2. What is the defining characteristic of select agents, according to the author?

3. In the author's opinion, can scientists actually create highly infectious viruses from scratch?

I rise today in support of S. 485, the Select Agent Program and Biosafety Improvement Act of 2009. . . .

Elevating the Priority of the Biological Weapons Threat

This bill will enhance our nation's biosecurity and improve the biosafety of our most secure laboratories. We must do everything we can to make sure that biological agents and toxins that could present a serious threat to public health are kept safe and secure in containment laboratories and out of the hands of terrorists.

In December 2008, 6 months after we introduced this legislation for the first time, the bipartisan Commission on the Prevention of WMD [weapons of mass destruction] Proliferation and Terrorism reported it is "more likely than not" that a weapon of mass destruction will be used in a terrorist attack by the end of 2013. The commission's report, *World at Risk*, found that terrorists are more likely to obtain and use a biological weapon than a nuclear weapon and, therefore, the U.S. government should make bioterrorism a higher priority. According to the report, "Only by elevating the priority of the biological weapons threat will it be possible to bring about substantial improvements in global biosecurity." Many of the specific recommendations contained in that report are reflected in this legislation.

S. 485 achieves two overarching goals. First, it reauthorizes and improves the Select Agent Program. This program was created in the 1990s to control the transfer of certain dangerous biological agents and toxins that could be used for bioterrorism. The program expanded after the anthrax attacks in 2001; however, the authorization expired at the end of September 2007.

Ensuring the Safety of Biodefense

Second, the bill evaluates and enhances the safety and oversight of high containment laboratories. These laboratories are used by scientists to study select agents and other infectious materials. Labs are categorized by their safety level. There are four levels, termed Biosafety Level—BSL—1 through 4, with 4 being the highest level. The number of these labs has grown, both domestically and internationally, in the last several years.

The Select Agent Program is jointly administered by the U.S. Department of Health and Human Services' (HHS) Centers for Disease Control and Prevention—CDC—and the U.S. Department of Agriculture's—USDA—Animal and Plant Health Inspection Service—APHIS. The program was intended to prevent terrorism, and protect public and animal health and safety, while not hampering important life-saving research. This is an obvious struggle that requires careful consideration, particularly when science is rapidly advancing around the globe.

Under the USA PATRIOT Act, it is illegal to possess "select agents" for reasons other than legitimate research. The Public Health Security and Bioterrorism Preparedness and Response Act of 2002 further required laboratories and laboratory personnel to undergo background checks by the FBI [Federal Bureau of Investigation] prior to approval for possession of select agents. As of February 2009, there are 82 select agents, meaning the agents pose a severe threat to public or animal health and safety. Thirteen of these agents are found naturally in the United States. There are 336 entities and 10,463 individuals registered with the CDC to work with select agents and toxins, and 64 entities and 4,149 individuals registered with APHIS.

A Comprehensive Evaluation
of the Program

We take four key actions in S. 485 to strengthen the Select Agent Program.

First, our legislation reauthorizes the program through 2014 and calls for a comprehensive evaluation of the program. The review, to be conducted by the National Academy of Sciences, will look at the effects of the program on international scientific collaboration and domestic scientific advances. This is timely because the WMD Commission recently suggested the need for an interagency review of the Select Agent Program and its impact on biological security and legitimate scientific research. Historically, the United States has been an international leader in biosecurity. In fact, last year [2008] Canada proposed legislation to tighten safety and access to pathogens and toxins of concern for bioterrorism. Canada's legislation, which was reintroduced earlier this month [February 2009], would establish a mandatory licensing system to track human pathogens, similar to our Select Agent Program. It also ensures compliance with the country's Laboratory Biosafety Guidelines across the country.

Second, the bill ensures a comprehensive list of select agents. Currently, CDC and APHIS develop a list of agents and toxins to which the program regulations apply. However, we believe some additional factors should be considered in revising the list. For example, scientific developments now make it possible to create agents from scratch or to modify them and make them more deadly. Highly infectious viruses or bacteria that are otherwise difficult to obtain can now be created by scientists.

In 2002, U.S. researchers assembled the first synthetic virus using the genome sequence for polio. Later, in 2005 scientists reconstructed the 1918 Pandemic Influenza virus. Then in January 2008, "safe" form of Ebola was created synthetically. While this "safe" Ebola can be used for legitimate research to

The Two-Edged Sword

The growth of [Biosecurity Level] BSL-3 and BSL-4 laboratories has raised concerns about the potential for pathogen release into local communities, as well as biological weapon proliferation, either through the transfer of pathogens or the transfer of technical knowledge through training and employment of foreign scientists in such venues. Events such as laboratory infections with select agents, improper shipping of select agents, and performance of research at inadequate biosafety levels have led policy makers to reexamine the current oversight framework. . . .

Increased high-containment laboratory capacity is a two-edged sword. Expansion allows for a greater diversity of biodefense research, more efficient public health sample testing, and more research discoveries. However, the increase in laboratories also increases the potential for theft or accidental release of dangerous pathogens and transfer of technical knowledge to persons wishing to do harm.

Frank Gottron and Dana A. Shea,
"Oversight of High-Containment Biological Laboratories:
Issues for Congress," Congressional Research Service,
March 5, 2009.

develop drugs and vaccines to protect against it, a scientist could also change it back to its lethal form. Also, earlier this year, advancements in technology yielded the first synthetic bacterial genome.

We must consider these scientific advances, including genetically modified organisms and agents created synthetically, if we are to address all agents of concern. In addition, DHS's

[Department of Homeland Security's] recent bioterrorism risk assessments provide new information for our assessment of biological threats. This information should also be considered when determining which agents and toxins should be regulated.

Next, the bill encourages sharing information with state officials to enable more effective emergency state planning. State health officials are currently not made aware of which agents are being studied within their state. This leaves medical responders, public health personnel, and animal health officials unprepared for a potential release, whether accidental or intentional.

Lastly, S. 485 clarifies the statutory definition of smallpox. The Intelligence Reform and Terrorism Prevention Act of 2004 criminalized the use of variola virus, the agent that causes smallpox. The statutory definition of the virus includes agents that are 85 percent identical to the causative strain. Researchers are worried this could be interpreted to also include the safer strain used to develop the smallpox vaccine, as well as less harmful naturally occurring viruses. This sort of ambiguity could be detrimental to necessary medical countermeasure research and development. Our bill requires the attorney general to issue guidance clarifying the interpretation of this definition.

Enhancing the Safety and Oversight of High Containment Laboratories

In addition, in this legislation we take three key actions to evaluate and enhance the safety and oversight of high containment laboratories.

First, our bill evaluates existing oversight of BSL-3 and -4, or high-containment, labs. The bill requires an assessment of whether current guidance on infrastructure, commissioning, operation, and maintenance of these labs is adequate. As I mentioned, the number of these labs is increasing around the globe. As these new facilities age, we need to make sure they are appropriately maintained. It is essential that laboratory workers and the public can be assured that these facilities are as safe as possible. If the guidance we currently have in place is not adequate, then we need to know how to improve it. In addition, the recent report by the WMD Commission called for HHS and DHS to lead an interagency effort to tighten government oversight of high-containment labs.

Second, the bill improves training for laboratory workers. The WMD Commission report also called for standard biosafety and biosecurity training for all personnel who work in high-containment labs and funding the development of such educational materials. As the number of laboratories and personnel increases, we must ensure workers are appropriately trained. Accidents and injuries in the lab such as chemical burns and flask explosions may result from improper use of equipment. Our bill develops a set of minimum standards for training laboratory personnel in biosafety and biosecurity, and encourages HHS and USDA to disseminate these training standards for voluntary use in other countries.

Finally, the bill establishes a voluntary Biological Laboratory Incident Reporting System. This system will encourage personnel to report biosafety and biosecurity incidents of concern and thereby allow us to learn from one another. Similar to the Aviation Safety Reporting System, which gathers information on aviation accidents, this system will help identify trends in biosafety and biosecurity incidents of concern and develop new protocols for safety and security improvements. Lab exposures to pathogens not on the select agent list will also be captured through this type of voluntary reporting system. The WMD Commission recommended promoting a culture of security awareness in the life sciences community and establishing whistleblower mechanisms within the life sciences community so that scientists can report their concerns about safety and security without risk of retaliation. We believe such a reporting system would help fulfill this recommendation.

In closing, I encourage my Senate colleagues to join Senator [Edward] Kennedy and me as we work to improve our nation's biosecurity and biosafety systems by passing S. 485, the Select Agent Program and Biosafety Improvement Act of 2009. I want to thank the many researchers, scientists, and state health officials from across the country who shared with me and my staff their ideas, experiences, and recommendations. In this time of exciting scientific advances, we must ensure our laws and prevention programs are updated to reflect current conditions. In addition, we must remain vigilant in our efforts to protect the American people from bioterrorism. The Select Agent Program is an important part of ensuring the nation's safety and security, and I look forward to working with my colleagues to reauthorize and improve the program.

> "The security benefits of tracking pathogens are inherently limited, and the Select Agent Program may also inadvertently and negatively affect the progress of scientific research and international scientific collaborations."

Increased Regulations Regarding the Select Agent Program Could Undermine Valuable Research

Gigi Kwik Gronvall

Gigi Kwik Gronvall maintains in the following viewpoint that any enhancement for security purposes of the Select Agent Program should proceed with caution, keeping in mind that the pursuit of research to develop effective vaccines is of the utmost importance. Gronvall cites as an example that placing shipping restrictions on a biological agent could interfere with international research collaboration. Gronvall is a senior associate at the Center for Biosecurity of the University of Pittsburgh Medical Center. Her research goals include reducing the threat of biologi-

Gigi Kwik Gronvall, "Improving the Select Agent Program," *Bulletin of the Atomic Scientists*, October 29, 2008. Copyright © 2008 by the Educational Foundation for Nuclear Science, Chicago, IL, 60637. Reproduced by permission of Bulletin of the Atomic Scientists: The Magazine of Global Security News & Analysis.

cal warfare and improving responses to natural and deliberate biological outbreaks.

As you read, consider the following questions:

1. According to Gigi Kwik Gronvall, who has legal access to the "select" biological agents?

2. In the author's opinion, does research on pathogens present security risks?

3. Because most select agents grow naturally, is it relatively easy to monitor and track such pathogens, according to Gronvall?

Immediately following the 2001 anthrax attacks [involving delivery of the agent through the mail], U.S. officials didn't know how many U.S. research laboratories held stocks of *Bacillus anthracis*, the causative agent of anthrax disease. And they didn't know how many researchers within those labs that did have stocks had ready access to the strains. This complicated the investigation of the source of the material used in the attacks. In the seven intervening years, U.S. officials have improved this situation. As a consequence of an expanded Select Agent Program, they now monitor the possession and transfer of more than 70 viruses, bacteria, toxins, and rickettsia [bacteria] (including anthrax) that could theoretically be processed into bioweapons, in all U.S. government, academic, and private laboratories. By law, only individuals cleared by the Department of Justice have access to these "select" biological agents.

This increased accountability and security for pathogens is valuable, especially in light of FBI [Federal Bureau of Investigation] assertions that the anthrax used in 2001 came from a U.S. biodefense laboratory. However, the security benefits of tracking pathogens are inherently limited, and the Select Agent Program may also inadvertently and negatively affect the progress of scientific research and international scientific collaborations. As the U.S. Congress considers legislation to reauthorize the Select Agent Program, it should take steps to evaluate and fine-tune the program to provide maximum benefits to security while promoting scientific advances. Research on pathogens certainly presents risks, but the greater risk is in not pursuing the research, and failing to develop effective vaccines and medicines to prevent and treat disease.

The Program's Origins

The Select Agent Program was launched by the Antiterrorism and Effective Death Penalty Act of 1996, which prohibited the transfer of some "select" agents from one laboratory to another without registration with the CDC [Centers for Disease Control and Prevention]. Congress passed the law in response to the difficulties in prosecuting Larry Wayne Harris, a member of the white supremacist group Aryan Nations, who in 1995 legally obtained *Yersinia pestis*, the causative agent of plague, from American Type Culture Collection [ATCC], a biological services company. The 2001 USA PATRIOT Act and the Public Health Security and Bioterrorism Preparedness and Response Act of 2002 strengthened accountability and restrictions for access to agents on the select agent list.

The program primarily involves three government agencies: the Animal and Plant Health Inspection Service (APHIS) at the Department of Agriculture, the Centers for Disease Control and Prevention (CDC) at the Department of Health and Human Services; and the Department of Justice. The CDC regulates some select agents such as Ebola virus and APHIS is the sole regulator of others such as foot-and-mouth virus. Some agents such as anthrax are "overlap" agents, which can be regulated by either CDC or APHIS. These agencies also inspect the facilities where the select agents are researched.

The Program's Limitations

As of April [2008], 9,918 people were approved to work with select agents through CDC, and 4,336 through APHIS. As of

May 2, 2008, 324 entities, including government agencies, academic institutions, corporations, societies, and sole proprietorships, were registered with the CDC select agent program. Though officials have strengthened pathogen security measures since 2001, a range of factors inherently limit the effectiveness of the Select Agent Program:

- **The program is U.S. centered.** It is a criminal offense in the United States to possess select agents, unless for bona fide medical, clinical, or research purposes, yet laboratories outside the United States are not governed by the same rules.

- **Most select agents are naturally occurring.** With the exception of the smallpox virus and the 1918 flu virus, all select agents can be found in nature, in hospital laboratories, or in sick people and animals. For example, *Burkholderia pseudomallei*, the causative agent of melioidosis, is endemic in Southeast Asia and Northern Australia; viral equine encephalitis occasionally appears in Central and South America; plague bacteria is presently causing the collapse of prairie dog colonies in the western United States; and *Bacillus anthracis* is found in laboratories and soil all over the world.

- **Tracking individual pathogens is extremely difficult.** Living organisms grow and multiply. Miniscule amounts of a pathogen could be sufficient to produce tons of pathogenic cultures.

- **New technologies can circumvent the need to acquire select agents from a laboratory.** In 2002, researchers at SUNY [State University of New York] Stony Brook reported that they constructed poliovirus from short laboratory-synthesized sequences of DNA. Since then, DNA synthesis technologies have dramatically improved, and many more select agents are within reach of being synthetically created.

Some Scientists Pass up Risks and Stall the Research

The American Society for Microbiology is holding firm on the principle of publishing enough details of an experiment to allow other scientists to try to repeat the work. It reiterated its policy after several scientists submitting papers to the society's journals asked that fine details of their experiments be left unpublished for fear that they could be misused.

"This is going to grow into a major debate in the scientific community," predicted [bioterrorism expert Ronald] Atlas of the microbiology society. "If restrictions are reasonable and responsible, they're just fine. If they get too draconian, they'll chill science."

In many ways, the chilling process has already begun. It is driven in part by the scientists themselves, who have found that it may be wiser in these less innocent times to destroy samples and restrict themselves rather than risk a bureaucratic or legal nightmare. . . .

Rosie Mestel,
"In the Lab, Suspicion Spreads,"
Los Angeles Times, *August 28, 2002.*

- **New potential agents are not on the list.** A recent report from the National Science Advisory Board for Biosecurity warns, "It is increasingly easy to produce synthetic genomes that encode novel and taxonomically unclassified agents with pathogenic properties equivalent to, or possibly more harmful than, current select agents." In other words, advances in synthetic genomics and synthetic biology could lead to new pathogens that will not easily fit into an oversight framework.

Research Delays and Criminal Penalties

In addition to these challenges, the Select Agent Program could present roadblocks in the event of a public health crisis. In 2004, a group of 13 scientists wrote a letter to the CDC asking that the SARS [severe acute respiratory syndrome] virus be kept off the select agent list because they feared that adding the virus to the list would hinder important research. Indeed, placing the virus on the list would have caused research delays—researchers would have needed to be cleared by the Department of Justice, a process that takes about 45 days—in the midst of a public health crisis. Placing an agent on the select list requires some laboratories to make expensive security upgrades to protect the agent from theft, loss, or unauthorized access, and the facilities would need to be inspected by the CDC. Shipping restrictions for transferring samples from one laboratory to another could also interfere with international collaborations, and running afoul of the law could result in up to $250,000 in fines for an individual and $500,000 for a research institution for each select agent violation. Criminal penalties could include imprisonment for up to 5 years.

Observers blame the fear of violating the law for a decrease in the number of samples that clinical laboratories send to research universities. If scientists at a clinical laboratory identify a select agent, they have a week to transfer it or destroy it; too often, it is easier to destroy the sample than to fill out all the necessary forms and take the risk that criminal penalties could result from doing it improperly.

The Importance of the Research Mission

The limitations of tracking pathogens suggest that the Select Agent Program can be only one part of U.S. biodefense efforts. Additional oversight and accountability measures may strengthen the Select Agent Program, but it will be important to balance gains in security with the need to pursue scientific advances that lead to the development of medical counter-measures against biological weapon threats. Legislation introduced in the 110th Congress, the Select Agent Program and Biosafety Improvement Act of 2008 (S. 3127 and H.R. 6671), asks the National Academy of Sciences to evaluate how the Select Agent Program has enhanced biosecurity and biosafety and what effect it has had on international scientific collaboration and scientific advances. This could be an excellent opportunity to evaluate how important research can proceed as securely as possible.

The FBI investigation into the 2001 anthrax letters suggests it is possible for one person to produce a lethal bioweapon without specific training and without specialized equipment. In the face of this security dilemma, it is imperative to develop new medical countermeasures such as vaccines and drugs, diagnostic tests, and cost-effective approaches to decontaminating physical structures. While restricting access to pathogens in laboratory stocks is important, any additional security for select agents needs to proceed with caution and knowledge of the program's limitations in order to protect the research mission.

"The U.S. health care delivery sector is not equipped or prepared to provide timely medical care to the tens or possibly even hundreds of thousands of casualties that could result from a successful bioattack."

The U.S. Government Should Invest More for Epidemic Preparedness

Tara O'Toole

In the following viewpoint, Tara O'Toole maintains that terrorist groups are fully capable of attacking the United States using covert biological warfare tactics, which could result in epidemics of infectious disease. She further maintains that the U.S. health care system is ill-equipped to handle the magnitude of victims that could result from a bioterrorist attack and, therefore, needs increased federal funding to improve its medical preparedness capabilities. O'Toole is the director and chief executive officer of the Center for Biosecurity of the University of Pittsburgh Medical Center and professor of medicine at the University of Pittsburgh Medical School.

Tara O'Toole, "Testimony Before the U.S. House of Representatives Committee on Appropriations, Subcommittee on Homeland Security, Hearing on Bioterrorism Preparedness and the Role of DHS Chief Medical Officer," Center for Biosecurity, University of Pittsburgh Medical Center, March 29, 2007. Reproduced by permission of the author.

As you read, consider the following questions:

1. In the author's opinion, what technical barriers do terrorists face in seeking to conduct biological attacks?

2. Because of the extreme difficulty in detecting and preventing bioterrorist attacks, what must defense efforts rely on, according to Tara O'Toole?

3. Why are epidemics of infectious disease sometimes termed "terrorism in slow motion," according to the author?

This committee [U.S. House of Representatives Committee on Appropriations], I believe, has a unique opportunity to consider "homeland security" from a strategic perspective. The complexity of "homeland security" missions and the number and diversity of programs and offices within the Department of Homeland Security (DHS) make such strategic thinking very difficult. But it is critically important that the Congress identify those "homeland security" activities and capabilities that are most critical to protecting national security, both for the near term and for the future. This requires that Congress understand the most likely and potentially most destabilizing threats that might arise either from natural causes or from the actions of "a thinking enemy." Wherever possible, we should strive to implement defenses that make the country not only safer, but stronger and more competitive. . . .

A covert bioterror attack on U.S. civilians or, even worse, a campaign of such attacks, is within the capability of terrorist groups today and could potentially cause tens of thousands of casualties and immense social and economic disruption. The scope and seriousness of the bioterror threat has been emphasized and verified by multiple U.S. government agencies and analyses. DHS's own Probabilistic Threat Assessment of Biological Agents is a well-done technical analysis of the biothreat. I urge every member of this committee to be briefed on this assessment and to be familiar with the national security implications of this analysis.

Lethality of Biological Weapons

The lethality of biological weapons mirrors that of nuclear weapons. Nothing else—not large conventional explosions, not chemical weapons, and not radiation devices—is in the same class. In 1993, the Congressional Office of Technology Assessment determined that 100 kilograms of aerosolized anthrax released upwind of Washington, D.C., under favorable weather conditions would cause 1 to 3 million deaths—approximately the same number of casualties that would result from a one megaton hydrogen bomb dropped on the city. A subsequent analysis by the World Health Organization posited similar death tolls from a biological attack.

Biological weapons have been proven to work on a large scale by U.S. testing in the South Pacific in the 1960s and 70s. We know now that the former Soviet Union had a massive bioweapons program that employed 40,000 people at its height and manufactured hundreds of tons of powdered anthrax and smallpox annually. This secret program was largely invisible until defectors detailed its existence.

It is important to recognize that the technical barriers to building bioweapons that faced the superpowers in the 1970s have been overtaken by the rapid advancements in bioscience. There are today no significant technical barriers to terrorists seeking to conduct large-scale bioattacks. As the Defense Science Board wrote in June 2001, "major impediments to the development of biological weapons—strain availability, weaponization technology, and delivery technology—have been largely eliminated in the last decade by the rapid global spread of biotechnology."

Difficulty in Detecting Biological Weapons

Al Qaeda is known to be seeking biological weapons, and according to the Robb-Silberman Commission's report on WMD [weapons of mass destruction] Intelligence Capabilities, evidence gathered in Afghanistan demonstrated that al Qaeda's efforts to develop bioweapons were more advanced than had been expected. In 2004, the U.S. National Intelligence Council declared, "Our greatest concern is that terrorists might acquire biological agents, or less likely, a nuclear device, either of which could cause mass casualties."

The ease with which bioweapons programs can be hidden and the lack of any definitive intelligence "signatures" indicative of illicit bioweapons activity are some of the reasons why these "asymmetric" weapons are attractive to terrorists. The materials and know-how needed to build a powerful bioweapon have legitimate "dual-use" [technology that can be used for legitimate public health needs such as vaccines and also for biological warfare] applications, making it very difficult to identify or track bioterrorist plans and preparations. We cannot count on identifying and interdicting would-be bioterrorists before they strike, and, as the 2001 anthrax attacks demonstrated, it is extremely difficult to assign attribution for such attacks once they occur. This means that traditional deterrence, which rests on certain and severe retribution, might be less effective against bioterrorist threats.

The extreme difficulty of detecting or interdicting bioterrorist efforts means that defense against covert bioterror attacks must rest on the nation's ability to diminish the death, suffering, and economic and social disruption that could result from bioattacks. This harsh truth is presumably the insight behind the dramatic increase in biodefense spending that began in 2002—federal spending on civilian biodefense went from approximately $250 million in FY[fiscal year]2002 to nearly $4 billion in FY2003; funding levels overall have remained more or less constant since. These sums are significant when measured against other spending programs in the Department of Health and Human Services, which presides over most "biodefense" initiatives. Four billion dollars per year does not seem like so much money if one compares this amount to sums routinely spent on national security programs in the Department of Defense. The important questions, of course, are: Is the country getting the defense against bioattacks that we need with the programs we have? Could we do better?

Terrorism in Slow Motion

Bioterrorist attacks result in epidemics of infectious disease, which differ from the results of other crises or other forms of terrorism. Epidemics have been called "terrorism in slow motion" because they unfold over a period of days and even weeks. It is not immediately clear how big an epidemic is or will become; it may be impossible to discern quickly if there has been a single attack or several. Many questions will confront leaders struggling to manage a bioattack: Who has been infected, who is at risk, where are the needed resources, where are they located now, and how might they be deployed to best effect?

The confusion that inevitably accompanies epidemics—whether they are naturally occurring or the result of a deliberate attack—is not easily resolved. Attaining sufficient "situational awareness" to make informed decisions about what to do will be a major challenge for decision makers at all levels. In the current U.S. health care system, it will probably be extremely difficult to even obtain an accurate, near real-time count of infected victims during a bioattack because rapid diagnostic tests and digital connections between public health and hospitals are lacking.

In addition to maintaining situational awareness, the other key epidemic response capabilities include the capacity to care

Emergency Care Is in Crisis

Both 9/11 [2001 terrorist attacks] and [2005 Hurricane] Katrina, and even the war in Iraq, serve as snapshots of how poorly prepared, coordinated, staffed and capable emergency and trauma care are to respond to our greatest needs. While government think tanks and policy effectors struggle with how to design a response for the next disaster, little attention is paid to the substantial data and numerous reports that show what emergency care facilities can be on a day-to-day basis: overloaded and crowded with non-emergencies, diverting ambulances, and boarding critical patients for days to gain access to hospitals. As the basic foundation of the "safety net," emergency care is in need of major resuscitation and an infusion of resources. To expect our emergency and trauma centers to shoulder the load in a disaster of 200, 2,000, or more patients under the current conditions is unrealistic . . . and dangerous for us all.

C. William Schwab,
Testimony Before the U.S. House of Representatives
Committee on Oversight and Government Reform,
"The State of Emergency Care for America:
At the Breaking Point, in Need of Resuscitation
and Going Nowhere," June 22, 2007.

for the sick; the ability to "protect the well"—to prevent contagious diseases from spreading, to immunize the population against future attacks, and to protect infected (but not yet symptomatic) persons; the capacity to deliver effective medical countermeasures (medicines and vaccines); and the capacity to constructively engage the cooperation and collaboration of citizens in epidemic response.

Incapability of the Health Care System

The DHS Office of the Chief Medical Officer has proposed taking responsibility to prepare medical response Conduct of Operations ("conops") plans for the major disaster scenarios DHS has judged to be highest priority. In my view, this is a critical task that is long overdue.

The U.S. health care delivery sector is not equipped or prepared to provide timely medical care to the tens or possibly even hundreds of thousands of casualties that could result from a successful bioattack. No municipality could care for a sudden flood of even 500 victims with inhalational anthrax—there simply is not enough "surge capacity" in today's financially stressed health care system to handle this load. The problem of lack of medical surge capacity is not specific to bioterrorist attacks. Nearly every type of terrorist attack or large-scale natural disaster would impose significant demands on health care facilities. At a March 15, 2007, meeting of medical and public health experts sponsored by the White House Homeland Security Council, attendees warned that the U.S. health care system would likely "collapse" in such events.

Yet, as we saw in the response to Hurricane Katrina, there is no national doctrine or operational plan that guides how health care facilities should prepare for or react to such calamities. Astonishingly, more than five years after high grade anthrax was mailed to members of Congress and the media, there is no conduct of operations plan for how the U.S. health care system would cope with the casualties of an anthrax attack. This is the case even though a bioterrorist attack is the mass casualty scenario judged by the National Intelligence Council to be "of greatest concern."

Underfunding of Hospital Preparedness

The federal government has not proposed or endorsed a coherent strategy or conduct of operations plan for medical response to mass casualty events, and has not adequately funded even minimal hospital preparedness activities. Responsibility and accountability for medical preparedness and response during large-scale catastrophes within HHS [the Department of Health and Human Services] and DHS are unclear, and in both agencies these functions are grossly understaffed and underfunded.

The Department of Health and Human Services (HHS) has provided modest funding for hospital preparedness since 2002, but much of this money has failed to reach hospitals; in any case, the amounts appropriated are small—about the cost of a single nurse's salary per year for each of the 5,000-plus hospitals in the country. The Center for Biosecurity has estimated that it would cost at least $5 billion annually ([up to] $1 million per hospital) to prepare hospitals for pandemic flu—this is exclusive of the costs of stockpiling supplies Dr. Dennis O'Leary, the CEO of the Joint Commission (formerly the Joint Commission on Accreditation of Healthcare Organizations) has stated that $1 million might improve preparedness at a small, 20-bed hospital, but would likely be inadequate for large, urban medical centers, which might require as much as $10 million annually for disaster preparedness.

Interpreting this minimal funding and relative lack of federal guidance as a signal that hospital disaster preparedness is a low priority, many hospitals have conducted only minimal disaster planning. Few hospitals have created regional plans for collaborating with other hospitals in their jurisdiction. Those medical centers that have formed regional planning groups have had difficulty communicating with other regions or spreading lessons learned.

A major problem is the lack of a recognized "organizing authority" with the standing to induce independent, competitive hospitals to engage in joint planning and to collaborate in crises. Most mayors and governors are unaware of the importance of regional hospital collaborations for emergencies in part because the hospital system is largely in private hands and not part of the government, and partly because America has not experienced many "mass casualty events."

These facts make the need for a coherent medical mass casualty response all the more urgent and necessary. Although it would be desirable going forward to clarify the medical response authorities and responsibilities of DHS versus those of HHS, the current pressing need is to produce a coherent, national conduct of operations plan for mass medical casualty events. Such an effort should proceed with a great deal of stakeholder involvement and collaboration. A Mass Casualty Medical Response Conops Plan cannot be successfully created or imposed by the federal government without significant involvement of medical professionals and hospital leaders around the country. Many preparedness efforts underway in some regions are worthy of emulation and provide valuable lessons, as does our experience with medical response during Hurricane Katrina.

Periodical Bibliography

The following articles have been selected to supplement the diverse views presented in this chapter.

Bob Graham   "Bioterrorism—a Preventable Catastrophe," *Boston Globe*, December 18, 2008.

Gigi Kwik Gronvall   "Biodefense Countermeasures: The Impact of Title IV of the U.S. Pandemic and All-Hazards Preparedness Act," *Emerging Health Threats Journal*, 2008.

Elaine M. Grossman   "Science Groups Counter WMD Panel's Prescription for Stemming Biological Threats," Global Security Newswire, March 13, 2009.

Barry Kellman   "Report Card: Biological Terrorism," Partnership for a Secure America, August 28, 2008.

Anthony L. Kimery   "Crisis in Mass Casualty Medical Care," *Homeland Security Today*, May 20, 2008.

John Dudley Miller   "Postal Anthrax Aftermath: Has Biodefense Spending Made Us Safer?" *Scientific American*, November 6, 2008.

Randall Murch   "How to Prevent the Next Biological Agent Attack," *Bulletin of the Atomic Scientists*, August 14, 2008.

Monica Schoch-Spana   "Community Resilience for Catastrophic Health Events," *Biosecurity and Bioterrorism*, 2008.

John D. Solomon   "It's an Emergency. We're Not Prepared," *Washington Post*, May 18, 2008.

How Can Biological
Warfare Be Prevented?

Chapter Preface

In her June 2007 article, "The Threat of Bioweapons," in *American Thinker*, Janet Ellen Levy argued that "the ultimate goal of bioterrorism is to induce fear, panic, and chaos by high morbidity and mortality rates to break down the existing political, economic, and social structure." "For bioweapons to be successful," she continued, "the biological agent should consistently produce the desired effect of death or disease." Following that line of thinking, if a nation were well-prepared and able to defend against a biological warfare attack so that such panic, chaos, and high mortality rates would not occur, that fact alone might deter terrorists and thus prevent an attack from happening in the first place. To that end, many experts believe that the development of effective countermeasures or vaccines is instrumental in the prevention of biological warfare, and therefore the United States should vigorously pursue such vaccination programs.

The pursuit of medical countermeasures to prevent bioterrorism is not a new concept. In 2004, President George W. Bush signed into law the Project BioShield program and allocated $5.6 billion to procure vaccinations and drugs for the national stockpile. Major pharmaceutical companies and private investors, however, have shown little interest in the BioShield program, partially because the cost of drug development is high and the profits are low. Furthermore, medical countermeasures degrade over time and must be replenished periodically, which explains to some extent why the United States still does not have adequate supplies of anthrax vaccine stockpiled to immunize the population, even after the anthrax letter attacks in 2001.

Another major problem in developing biological warfare countermeasures is the long list of naturally occurring organisms that are potential weapons. Creating a vaccine for every specific pathogen—a policy often referred to as "one bug, one drug"—is considered by experts to be a short-sighted, expensive, and futile biodefense approach. Rather, they assert, countermeasure research should focus on broad spectrum remedies that work against many different bacteria and viruses. According to Tara O'Toole, director and chief executive officer of the Center for Biosecurity of the University of Pittsburgh Medical Center, the threat environment is too large to narrowly focus on a few diseases: "The United States does not yet have a coherent biodefense strategy, nor do we have a strategy for countermeasure research, development, and production that takes into account the full spectrum of possible bioweapons agents, including engineered threats." Some biodefense researchers, however, are currently delving into the possibility of creating vaccines that will stimulate an individual's immune system response to a wide variety of bacterial and viral pathogens.

Most national defense experts agree that the more robust and effective medical response capability a nation has, the more confident and resilient its citizens are, thus making that nation unattractive as a target for terrorists hoping to inflict mass chaos and death. The development of an effective vaccination program is one approach in preventing bioterrorism. The authors in this chapter discuss this and other ideas on how to prevent terrorists from resorting to biological warfare.

| "The strengthening of the Biological Weapons Convention offers the single best hope of global restraints."

The United States Should Strengthen Its Commitment to the Biological Weapons Convention

Jeanne Guillemin

Jeanne Guillemin maintains in the following viewpoint that the proliferation of biological weapons represents a serious global problem—so much so that a system of restraints such as the Biological Weapons Convention (BWC) must be adhered to globally. She further maintains that the United States should assume a leadership role in the BWC and set an example of cooperation and transparency with regard to biomedical technology. Guillemin, a professor of sociology at Boston College, has written extensively about infectious diseases and biological weapons controversies.

Jeanne Guillemin, *Biological Weapons: From the Invention of State-Sponsored Programs to Contemporary Bioterrorism*. New York: Columbia University Press, 2005. Copyright © 2005 Columbia University Press. All rights reserved. Republished with permission of the Columbia University Press, 61 W. 62nd St., New York, NY 10023.

As you read, consider the following questions:

1. In the author's opinion, what was the core reason for the U.S. government's rejection of a strengthened Biological Weapons Convention (BWC)?

2. What is the best protection against the proliferation of biological weapons, according to Jeanne Guillemin?

3. In the author's opinion, why does the United States bear a special responsibility to promote long-term restraints against biological weapons?

Biology today is as susceptible to hostile exploitation as were chemistry in World War I and physics in World War II. The formidable power of international commerce is behind this basic science, moving it toward innovations that, along with marketable medical value, might also be turned to destructive ends. If exploited by states, the science and technology of biological weapons could pose one of the most serious problems humanity has ever faced. A new generation of biological weapons, if pursued with vigor, could make them technologically competitive, especially for human control and domination. Unless the power of biotechnology is politically restrained, it could introduce scientific methods that would change the way war is waged and increase the means for victimizing civilians.

A Question of Sufficient Restraints Against Biological Warfare

The question at present is whether sufficient national and international restraints against this danger are in place, especially when scientific knowledge itself is at issue. In the past, various, at times serendipitous, combinations of legal norms, public oversight, technical obstacles, and political leadership prevented the use of biological weapons. Overall, though, the world has been lucky, in that influential political actors took action at critical junctures and that the general historical trend of the last century has been toward transparency and open government.

History shows that the problem of biological weapons proliferation is too complex to be solved by any single restraint. A reasoned assessment of threats and measures is the first step to resolving the problem of proliferation. This problem should be understood as potentially more serious now than in the past, in great measure because human malice coupled with human ingenuity is a constant in world history. History also tells us that without a long-term commitment to nonproliferation, we are gambling with the future.

A Question of Trust and Mistrust

The United States' definition of its interests sets a standard to which the rest of the world cannot help but react. Even before September 11 [2001 terrorist attacks] and the 2001 anthrax letter attacks, the United States was in retreat from new international initiatives to strengthen the Biological Weapons Convention (BWC), while it also reinforced its homeland security policies. The [George W.] Bush administration reinforced American unilateralism and a confrontational approach to international relations that, as in the Reagan era, depended on conspicuous military might. After September 11 [2001], "waging war on two fronts" was President Bush's apt description for America's militancy abroad and civil-defense orientation at home.

At the core of the US government's rejection of a strengthened BWC was the belief that the United States was exceptionally trustworthy and could therefore interpret and implement legal norms as it chose. Close allies of the United States, especially the United Kingdom, were trustworthy as well. In distinct contrast, suspect nations such as Iraq, North Korea, Libya, Syria, and Iran posed the most serious threat because they were too closed and perfidious to abide by law. Other states such as China, India, Pakistan, and later Russia were too well-armed and large to ignore but still not fully trusted.

This perception of a global division between "haves" and "have-nots" is often shared among advanced industrial nations and has influenced treaty negotiations on weapons of mass destruction. From this viewpoint, the world appears divided into "responsible" Western states that can be trusted with nuclear weapons and "irresponsible" non-Western states that cannot be trusted with the weapons they have or that must be prevented from acquiring any. In this view, arms control is but one element of a web of restraints imposed by the North on the South, encompassing export controls, strong biological and chemical defenses, and a "determined and effective" military response.

A competing political vision assumes inseparable common interests among all the world's states in reducing the threat of weapons of mass destruction and of war and violence in general. It holds that the benefits of biomedical technology should be shared between wealthy nations and those in economic need. This perspective promotes the international mobilization of citizens, including scientists and physicians, to promote the interdiction of biological weapons. Far from being antagonistic to American or Western values, this approach is based on openness and democratic participation, extended to a global context. It encourages nongovernmental and grassroots organizations and the idea of civil society as part of the long-term international solution to present dangers.

The dichotomy between the two approaches is less sharp than it may appear. Despite the forces of globalization, the importance of sovereign state governments and state law in reducing weapons proliferation endures. The initiatives of advanced industrial states can be vitally constructive, provided there are options for broader cooperation. International measures based on trust are likewise essential for persuading a

Promoting Transparency in Biotechnology

Transparency is an integral component of arms control. It can dispel concerns of noncompliance by reassuring actors that others are not misusing technologies or goods for hostile purposes. It can also deter actors from engaging in banned activities for fear that their activities will be exposed. In biological arms control, transparency is of pronounced importance because dual-use material, equipment, and knowledge are extensively embedded in contemporary biotechnology.

The potential for the abuse of these technologies increases each year as they become more advanced and diffuse. As the Department of State recently reported, "[T]he fact that biotechnology equipment and materials can be used interchangeably for peaceful or nefarious purposes, and the ease and speed by which illegal activities can be concealed make verification of compliance with the [Biological Weapons Convention (BWC)] an especially difficult challenge."

Nicolas Isla and Iris Hunger,
"BWC 2006: Building Transparency Through
Confidence Building Measures," July 1, 2006.

range of governments that openness through, for example, mutual on-site inspections and scientific partnership, is preferable to continued secrecy.

A Question of Secrecy

At present [2005] 151 nations are parties to the Biological Weapons Convention, and 132 nations are parties to the Geneva Protocol, a strong testimony to the international norm.

The BWC's lack of verification and compliance provisions is frequently referred to as its greatest shortcoming in reducing the threat of proliferation. What, then, is the solution?

US government objections to a protocol that would strengthen the treaty have been based on what it has argued is its exceptional need for military secrecy and the proprietary needs of its pharmaceutical industries. This double argument raises the question of whether, regarding this category of weapon, the safety of one nation is strictly divisible from all others, even, for example, from that of European allies like the United Kingdom, which have supported treaty compliance and transparency.

The US defensive program is the largest in the world, a fact that US representatives have often underscored. But how large and, more important, how secret should it be to serve national interests—which are fundamentally public interests—or those of its allies? The 1991 BWC Confidence-Building Measures, to which the US government agreed, require declarations of legitimate defensive projects and locales, leaving the substance of the classified work undisturbed. These declarations have compliance, not total transparency, as a goal. Further, they are intended as a means of distinguishing between legitimate programs and the illegitimate ventures that are more likely to be hidden and therefore undeclared. The United States should have no need for biological defense programs whose locations and general nature must be kept secret. But how much secrecy is too much?

If, as the covert CIA [Central Intelligence Agency] and Department of Defense projects suggest, the United States has a stake in undeclared projects at undeclared sites, it may be engaged in activities that increase the risks of proliferation and therefore danger to the public. With the world's largest military, the United States could set broad and dangerous standards for biological weapons research. Escalation within a defensive program, for example, could advance the laboratory and delivery technology for biological weapons. Small-scale, arbitrary projects such as those leaked to the press in 2001 could pave the way for new agents or for attack simulations on a large, elaborate scale, to second-guess what a suspected enemy might develop. In time, other states or organizations would gain access to the same or similar classified technology, whether for a new agent, drug, bomb, or missile.

The US presumption that the threat of biological weapons is foreign is generally supportable, but several domestic crimes, including the 2001 anthrax letters, point to risks within the United States, perhaps from its own programs. Intelligence and defense officials may want to explore what an adversary might do, but secret knowledge and materials generated by their own biodefense projects could be put to hostile use by the increasing numbers of Americans with access and special skills.

Transparency in the name of public safety need not require front-page headlines, but it does require oversight and accountability. Ample US military funding without civil review fueled biological weapons proliferation in the past, and it could pose a danger again. . . .

A Question of Global Transparency and Cooperation

When restraints on biological weapons break down, the risks of unprecedented danger increase. If history is our guide, the threat of biological weapons increases in direct proportion to government secrecy, closed military cultures, and a subsequent lack of accountability to the public.

Looking back at the last century, we can feel optimistic at the progress made thus far in deflecting the risks of biological weapons. The French returned to a biological warfare program after World War II and then abandoned it. The British left off their program in the late 1950s and became leaders in treaty negotiations. The horrific program of the Japanese

Army has had most of its secrets divulged and remains, with the Holocaust, one of the most distressing examples of barbarism within a great culture. The US offensive program is no more; the giant Horton Test Sphere at Fort Detrick is on the National Register as a Maryland tourist site. The totalitarian Soviet Union, a political mastodon, took its offensive program to its historical grave. Now international consensus against biological weapons can be weighed against the complexities of the new wars born of globalization, poverty, and ethnic and religious fanaticism. In all, the strengthening of the Biological Weapons Convention offers the single best hope of global restraints.

As before, the best protection against the proliferation of biological weapons is transparency. Biological weapons are indeed a different class of threat, one that is variable in scale, in source, in its many potential agents, and in its possible impact on communities, including psychological and social disruption as well as illness and death. A radical argument can be made regarding both biological weapons and bioterrorism: that the policy goal should be an unobstructed flow of reliable information, in public education, in the review of scientific research, in disease reporting and diagnosis, in forensic investigation, in intelligence, in government oversight, and in international treaty compliance measures. Military and intelligence agencies may balk and pharmaceutical corporations may protest. It is for government leaders to show that their first priority is the protection of public lives, without qualification.

By virtue of its power and its democratic tradition, the United States bears a special responsibility to promote comprehensive, long-term restraints against biological weapons. Government secrecy, as the twentieth century shows, caused a degradation of biology and increased mortal risk to unsuspecting civilian targets. The antidote to a reoccurrence of programs and threats worse than the ones of the past is the fostering of international relations that increase mutual trust and reduce the drastic economic inequalities that divide the world and obstruct communication.

The United States is uniquely suited to lead this mission, if it can reconfigure its role in a politically complex world where national defense requires international cooperation. In all matters of disease transmission, freely shared information is essential to our protection. As Senator Daniel Patrick Moynihan wrote in 1998, commenting on the end of years of Cold War secrecy and weapons proliferation, "Openness is now a singular, and singularly American, advantage." It is an advantage that can be too easily lost, in short-sighted homeland security policies and in failed relations with other nations, to our peril and the peril of future generations. In military history, biological weapons were a failed innovation. May they remain so.

"We reaffirm our commitment to the
[Biological Weapons] Convention and
underscore that it continues to serve as
an important international norm
against the use of biology as a weapon."

The United States Is Strongly Committed to the Biological Weapons Convention

John C. Rood

*In the following viewpoint, John C. Rood maintains that the
United States believes strongly in the global importance of the
Biological Weapons Convention (BWC) and will cooperate fully
in its commitment against biological warfare. Rood further maintains that the BWC needs to be strengthened; to that end, he
suggests that the BWC member states implement their own national measures to criminalize the development and proliferation
of biological weapons, promote disease surveillance, and enhance
biosecurity measures. Rood was the acting under secretary of
state for Arms Control and International Security in the George
W. Bush administration.*

John C. Rood, "Address to the Sixth Biological Weapons Convention Review Conference," U.S. Diplomatic Mission to the United Nations in Geneva, November 20, 2006.
geneva.usmission.gov.

As you read, consider the following questions:

1. What are the three major nonproliferation treaties, according to John C. Rood?

2. Is Syria a state party to the Biological Weapons Convention (BWC), according to the author?

3. In the author's opinion, is it possible for the same techniques used in biological research for the benefit of humans also be used to harm humans?

Over thirty years ago, the Biological Weapons Convention [BWC] entered into force as the key legal and normative barrier to the spread of biological weapons. The convention's condemnation of biological weapons "as repugnant to the conscience of mankind" holds as true today as it did when the BWC was signed in 1972.

The United States believes that the BWC today is strong. We reaffirm our commitment to the [Biological Weapons] Convention and underscore that it continues to serve as an important international norm against the use of biology as a weapon.

Yet the world is a very different place today than in 1972. During the Cold War, countries were concerned mostly about state-run programs. Now we also must recognize the grim prospect of terrorist organizations using biology as a weapon of terror and mass destruction, and we must gird ourselves to respond to new and evolving threats.

Confronting the Biological Weapons Threat

When states parties to the Biological Weapons Convention gathered at the resumed Fifth Review Conference in November 2002, the international effort to combat the biological weapons threat took a pragmatic and measurable step forward. States parties recognized the necessity of a three-pronged strategy of national, bilateral, and multilateral measures and unanimously adopted a tailored program of work to confront the biological weapons threat in today's strategic environment—in which threats come from rogue states and terrorists.

It is with these threats in mind that we must continue to strengthen our efforts and adapt our nonproliferation and counterproliferation tools to stop the development and transfer of biological weapons.

Of the three major multilateral nonproliferation treaties—the Nuclear Non-Proliferation Treaty (NPT) and the Chemical Weapons Convention (CWC) are the other two—the BWC is the first to conduct a second review in the post-9/11 [2001 terrorist attacks] world.

BWC states parties are uniquely situated to evaluate the impact of a program of work that was conceived recognizing that both the object and purpose of the convention and the strategic reality that innovative, multifaceted, and comprehensive approaches to contend with the proliferation of weapons of mass destruction are essential.

Working Together Against Biological Weapons Threats

While the United States believes we are making significant strides, much work remains to be done. As we review the operation of the BWC over the next three weeks [in late 2006], it is essential that each state party thoroughly examines the actions it is taking now, and the actions it needs to take in the future to exclude the possibility of biological agents and toxins being used as weapons.

The United States looks forward to discussing constructive and practical measures to combat the biological weapons threat. We seek to reinforce and thereby strengthen the BWC. We welcome a healthy and vigorous exchange of practical ideas.

Key Provisions of the Biological Weapons Convention (BWC)

Article	Provision
Article I	Never under any circumstances to acquire or retain biological weapons.
Article II	To destroy or divert to peaceful purposes biological weapons and associated resources prior to joining.
Article III	Not to transfer, or in any way assist, encourage or induce anyone else to acquire or retain biological weapons.
Article IV	To take any national measures necessary to implement the provisions of the BWC domestically.
Article V	To consult bilaterally and multilaterally to solve any problems with the implementation of the BWC.
Article VI	To request the UN [United Nations] Security Council to investigate alleged breaches of the BWC and to comply with its subsequent decisions.
Article VII	To assist States which have been exposed to a danger as a result of a violation of the BWC.
Article X	To do all of the above in a way that encourages the peaceful uses of biological science and technology.

TAKEN FROM: The Biological Weapons Convention, United Nations Office at Geneva.

We urge states to recognize the changes that have occurred in the global strategic environment and to avoid bringing up tired, old debates from the past and raising divisive ideological debates.

With regard to compliance, fundamental to the success of the BWC and its goal of ridding the world of biological weapons is full and effective compliance by all states parties. Noncompliance with the central obligation of the BWC poses a direct threat to international peace and security, and compliance concerns must be pursued vigorously. For this reason, such concerns must be raised not only at review conferences every five years, but addressed by states parties with urgency as they arise. For our part, since the last review conference, the United States has engaged several states through diplomatic channels on issues of possible noncompliance with Article I [which prohibits possession of biological weapons] and other BWC obligations.

Noncompliance with the fundamental requirement not to develop biological weapons is of paramount concern. It would be irresponsible to strengthen the superstructure of the convention and yet turn a blind eye to problems with the foundation itself. The U.S. has concerns with the actions of a number of states and we publicly detail our compliance concerns in an annual report to the U.S. Congress.

The activities of North Korea, Iran, and Syria are of particular concern given their support for terrorism and lack of compliance with their international obligations. Each of these countries was identified in the most recent edition of the U.S. noncompliance report published in August 2005.

We believe that the regime in Iran probably has an offensive biological weapons program in violation of the BWC. Similarly, we also believe North Korea has a biological warfare capability and may have developed, produced, and weaponized for use biological weapons, also in violation of the BWC. Finally, we remain seriously concerned that Syria—a signatory but not a party to the BWC—has conducted research and development for an offensive BW [biological weapons] program.

The U.S. understands that the problem of noncompliance with the BWC is difficult but it must be faced head-on. The international community must always remain vigilant and steadfast, and root out violators that undermine the integrity of the convention.

Implementing National Measures Against Biological Warfare Activities

As the agreements reached during the 2003–2005 BWC Work Program reinforced, each state party must do its individual part by implementing national measures at home.

When there are suspicions of illicit BW activities, the convention requires each state party be more than just watchful and determined. States parties are obligated to undertake national measures to implement the convention. Specifically, Article III prohibits states parties from providing sensitive technologies—either directly or indirectly—to any person, group, or country that might seek to acquire biological weapons. Furthermore, Article IV requires that states parties vigilantly regulate and monitor biological activities within their own country or in areas under their jurisdiction or control, and aggressively pursue and prosecute those who would seek to use disease as a weapon of terror, destruction, or death. These obligations necessitate that states parties implement effective export controls.

There is a clear international consensus that national measures are critical, particularly in our efforts to prevent the proliferation of WMD and their related materials. In 2004, the United Nations Security Council recognized the importance of the adoption and enforcement of effective export controls by requiring all states to criminalize proliferation under UN [United Nations] Security Council Resolution 1540. Resolution 1540 mandates that all states take and enforce effective measures to establish domestic controls that will prevent the proliferation of biological weapons and other weapons of mass destruction and their means of delivery.

The United States has taken several measures to implement its obligations under the BWC and Resolution 1540, and we reiterate our willingness to provide assistance to states parties to adopt national measures.

Increasing Membership Against Biological Warfare

While it is critical that we undertake a dedicated effort under the BWC umbrella to ensure that all BWC states parties fully implement their obligations, we must also undertake steps to bring into the community of nations foreswearing biological weapons those states that remain outside of the convention. . . .

With 155 states parties, membership in the BWC ranks substantially behind that of other multinational nonproliferation treaties. The Nuclear Non-proliferation Treaty has 188 states parties, while the Chemical Weapons Convention has 180 states parties. Although the UN General Assembly annually calls upon states to join the BWC, there has been no concerted universality effort and little expansion of BWC membership for many years.

Given the increased international concerns about the threat of biological weapons, the United States believes that at this review conference, states parties to the BWC should seize the opportunity to launch a strong universality campaign embodied in an agreed action plan.

In addition, we hope that during the article-by-article review performed over the coming weeks and in our final declaration, that BWC states parties will explicitly endorse the importance of national export control measures in fulfilling the obligations under the convention and fully commit to complying with UN Security Council Resolution 1540.

Addressing Biosecurity Concerns

I will now turn to our proposals with respect to the intersessional work program leading up to the Seventh Review Conference. The United States believes that the 2003–2005 Work Program was constructive. The upcoming intersessional period provides an opportunity to build upon the previous work program and further strengthen implementation of the convention. The United States thus supports a robust intersessional effort building on the proven formula of the 2003–2005 Work Program.

The United States will support meetings of technical experts in Geneva for key implementation areas. We believe that two of the topics addressed between 2003 and 2005 are clearly worthy of further consideration and progress, with a special emphasis on promoting cooperation in these areas. The first is disease surveillance. This was one of the most productive and well-attended meetings of the intersessional period. Subsequent emergence of the avian influenza threat has underscored the importance of national and international efforts to address infectious disease. The United States strongly favors continued effort in this area.

A second area worthy of follow-up effort is biosecurity, that is, the challenge of keeping dual-use equipment and biological materials secure from theft and misuse, especially with regard to terrorism. To enhance progress in this area, we would propose that special emphasis be placed on international cooperation and the closely linked issue of biosafety.

The United States has also identified two new areas for intersessional focus. With respect to national legislation to outlaw illicit BW activities, we believe that enforcement needs to be squarely addressed. Parties to the BWC have a shared interest in ensuring that non-state actors who might engage in BWC-prohibited activities are apprehended and prosecuted. We would therefore propose a session where experts would share experiences related to investigation and prosecution of BW-related crimes, particularly those involving international cooperation, and discuss possibilities of further future collaboration.

Another issue we believe should be addressed concerns codes of conduct related to national activities to prevent misuse of biological research. In the life sciences, the same techniques used to gain insight and understanding for the benefit of human health and welfare may also be used to create a new generation of BW agents. In this proposed session, states would report on steps that have been taken at the national level since the discussions in 2005 and discuss possibilities for international cooperation and coordination.

Establishing Constructive Review Conferences

The second element of the 2003–2005 intersessional effort was meetings of states parties. In this regard, the United States proposes that one-week meetings of states parties be convened annually from 2007 to 2010 to consider progress and follow up for the respective action plans on universality and national implementation. Political-level discussions could also be held at these annual meetings in connection with the experts' meetings convened that year.

In conclusion, . . . let me again encourage those attending this review conference to begin work in earnest on a robust, practical and focused program that advances the operation and national implementation of the BWC. The United States has identified proposals for consideration which we believe will garner significant support, and we look forward to discussions of other useful and constructive ideas for advancing work under the BWC umbrella.

We must not allow this review conference to be sidetracked into ideological debates or hijacked by the destructive agenda of proliferators. There are many practical and positive steps that we can take to strengthen the BWC on all levels, and it is imperative that we continue to cooperate to achieve this goal.

> "The destruction of remaining Variola stocks is an overdue step forward for global public health and security that will greatly reduce the possibility that this scourge will kill again, by accident or design."

All Known Stocks of the Smallpox Virus Should Be Destroyed

Edward Hammond

In the following viewpoint, Edward Hammond insists that there is no valid reason to retain stocks of the smallpox virus, especially because further research on smallpox does not require samples of the live virus. He further insists that possession of the virus should be treated as a crime against humanity. Hammond, an American policy researcher, has focused his work on biotechnology-related policy.

As you read, consider the following questions:

1. According to Edward Hammond, what are the two countries that still retain stocks of the smallpox virus?

Edward Hammond, "Should the U.S. and Russia Destroy Their Stocks of Smallpox Virus?" *British Medical Journal* (BMJ), vol. 334, April 14, 2007, p. 774. Copyright © 2007 British Medical Association. Reproduced by permission.

2. Has the World Health Organization (WHO) found credible evidence that some terrorist organizations have possession of the smallpox virus, according to the author?

3. In the author's opinion, is it clear which countries legally own the smallpox virus stocks that have been retained?

The World Health Organization is justly proud of the global effort that led to the eradication of smallpox; but the truth is that the job remains unfinished. Although it is almost 30 years since the last natural transmission of smallpox virus (*Variola*), laboratories in the United States and Russia retain virus stocks.

The destruction of remaining *Variola* stocks is an overdue step forward for global public health and security that will greatly reduce the possibility that this scourge will kill again, by accident or design. Although deploying modern scientific techniques such as genetic engineering on smallpox virus may be intellectually intriguing, the risks far outweigh the potential benefits.

In 1990, the US secretary of health and human services, Louis Sullivan, made a pledge on behalf of the US government. "There is no scientific reason not to destroy the remaining stocks of wild virus," he declared, "so I am pleased to announce today that after we complete our sequencing of the smallpox genome, the United States will destroy all remaining virus stocks." Although the genome was published in 1994, the US still hasn't honoured its commitment.

WHO member states concur that the virus stocks must be destroyed. For more than a decade, the US and Russia have paid lip service to the WHO consensus while trying to outmanoeuvre actual destruction of the virus. In 1999 Russia and the US balked at the World Health Assembly resolution calling on them to destroy the virus (resolution 49.10). Since then, both countries have accelerated smallpox research. Particularly

Concern over Smallpox Research

A US government biosecurity committee has proposed that domestic US legal restrictions on possession of variola virus be repealed. The de facto effect of this recommendation would be to legalize possession of variola virus. Although holding an exact copy of the entire virus in replication-competent form would remain subject to regulation, possession of large amounts of smallpox DNA and construction and manipulation of viruses almost genetically identical to smallpox (i.e. essentially composed of variola genes) would not be subject to legal controls or even reporting to the government. Such viruses could pose an international public health threat.

Lim Li Ching, "Health: WHO Board Urged to Act on Worrying Smallpox Research Trends," The Oakland Institute, January 30, 2007.

risky experiments are underway to create a monkey model of human smallpox infection. The US has also proposed genetic engineering experiments with the virus.

There Is No Reason to Retain the Virus

WHO's experts have agreed that no valid reason exists to retain smallpox virus stocks for DNA sequencing, diagnostic tests, or vaccine development. In 2006, WHO's experts concluded: "Sufficient sequence information on the virus was now available; no further research requiring access to live variola virus was considered essential." They also determined that "the number of detection and diagnostic systems for variola virus now available was adequate." Antivirals are not absolutely required because existing vaccines are effective and diagnostic tests are rapid and accurate. And WHO experts have recently suggested that drugs against smallpox could be developed without the dangerous US experiments with live smallpox virus intended to create an animal model of human infection. WHO advisers suggest that this could be accomplished through the far safer route of using monkeypox virus.

The US has recently made much of the possibility of smallpox in the hands of terrorists or "rogue states." Illicit stocks have been used to justify retention of US and Russian smallpox virus stocks. There is a fallacy lurking here because smallpox virus stocks are not necessary to respond to a smallpox outbreak. If smallpox reappeared, the virus would be readily available if needed for biomedical purposes.

The claims about illicit stocks have also not been supported by evidence. The loudest allegations were against Iraq, but the US belatedly admitted that it was wrong. There is no credible evidence that any terrorist organisation has smallpox virus. To acquire the virus terrorists would have to breach security at one of WHO's repositories. Producing quantities of weaponised smallpox is beyond the means of any known terrorist group.

The World Will Be Safer with the Complete Destruction of Smallpox

The US National Science Advisory Board for Biosecurity is currently discussing a proposal to weaken domestic legislation to permit US laboratories to synthesise and possess larger sequences of smallpox DNA. This will make its DNA easier to acquire and increase the range of dangerous experiments possible outside the official WHO virus repositories.

In 2005, the head of the WHO eradication effort, Donald Henderson, told the *Independent*: "The less we do with the smallpox virus and the less we do in the way of manipulation at this point I think the better off we are." Yet one unfortunate consequence of the US insistence that its smallpox virus is critical to its national security is that other countries may become convinced that they too must possess the virus and research into it. The smallpox strains in the WHO repositories in the US and Russia were deposited by various countries and were isolated all over the world. It is extremely unclear who legally owns the collections.

The decades-old eradication job of WHO will be completed, and the world will be safer, when the US and Russian smallpox virus stocks are finally destroyed. Recently, Africa has taken the lead at the World Health Assembly. Its health ministers see all too clearly what could happen if smallpox were to escape. Africa's efforts, with support from other developing regions, have put WHO member states into a position to do more than recall unfulfilled pledges when the World Health Assembly convenes in May 2007.

As memory of the horror of smallpox recedes and biotechnology advances, it is important to draw a firm line around *Variola*. Instead of courting disaster, we should seek to ensure that possession of this virus is treated as a crime against humanity. The key prerequisite to criminalising *Variola* is to destroy the existing stocks. It has been three decades coming, but it is time for WHO to push the button on the autoclave. Better late than too late.

| "*Destroying the virus would be irreversible and short sighted.*"

Known Stocks of the Smallpox Virus Should Be Retained for National Security

John O. Agwunobi

In the following viewpoint, John O. Agwunobi contends that because the malicious use of smallpox remains a global threat and because there are no safe and effective treatments against the disease, destroying the virus completely is ill-advised. He further contends that continued research using the live virus is vital to create new, safer, and more effective antiviral drugs in the event a smallpox epidemic should break out. Agwunobi served as the twelfth assistant secretary for health of the U.S. Department of Health and Human Services.

As you read, consider the following questions:

1. In the author's opinion, have all live smallpox virus stocks been either destroyed or transferred to World Health Organization authorized repositories?

2. Are smallpox vaccines that were used successfully in the past safe for all people, according to John O. Agwunobi?

3. Are effective antiviral drugs for smallpox infection currently available, according to the author?

Smallpox, one of the great killers in human history, remains dangerous. Malicious use of smallpox remains a threat because almost certainly clandestine stocks exist. Despite the 33rd World Health Assembly's endorsement of the recommendation that all countries should destroy all live smallpox virus stocks, or transfer them to World Health Organization authorised, maximum-containment repositories, we cannot be certain this is the case. The United States believes that the global community should avoid any action that would jeopardise the important research on *Variola* virus conducted at the two authorised repositories of the virus. Destroying the virus would be irreversible and short sighted, for the reasons spelt out below.

Smallpox poses an important public health risk, particularly since the population has no immunity and there are no safe, effective treatments. *Variola* virus released by mistake or intentionally would be a public health emergency of international concern, as the revised *International Health Regulations* (2005) recognises. It would require a coordinated international response because modern, rapid, mass movement of people and multifocal outbreaks could result in smallpox spreading widely. In part because of this threat, the World Health Assembly authorised retention of the official stocks of live virus in 1999 and again in 2002.

To mitigate the threat of smallpox, scientists in the US and elsewhere, under the auspices of WHO, are cooperating in open, time-limited research with live *Variola* virus. An international expert WHO advisory committee reviews the research and reports annually on its progress. The research

Some Facts About Smallpox

Smallpox (also called variola) is the only disease that has been completely wiped out throughout the world. Smallpox is also potentially one of the most devastating biological weapons ever conceived. . . .

Geopolitical events in the last decade and revelations concerning offensive biological warfare programs by certain foreign governments have raised concern that this virus may have fallen into the hands of other foreign states who might seek to use the virus as a biological weapon. . . .

Routine vaccination of the general population in the United States stopped after 1980. Vaccination of military personnel was discontinued in 1989. Researchers estimate that vaccinated people retain immunity for about 10 years, although the duration has never been fully evaluated. Therefore, the current population in the United States is considered vulnerable to smallpox. About 42% of the US population is younger than 30 years and has never been vaccinated.

eMedicineHealth, "Smallpox," 2005.
www.emedicinehealth.com.

agenda focuses on the need to improve diagnostics and to develop antiviral drugs and safer, effective vaccines against smallpox.

Safer and More Effective Vaccines and Antiviral Drugs

Vaccination was central to the successful eradication of smallpox. In the past, smallpox vaccines were made with live *Vaccinia* virus. However, these vaccines are contraindicated for various groups of the population because of illnesses such as cancer, HIV, heart problems, and dermatitis or treatment with immunocompromising therapies. Adverse reactions to the vaccine in these people can be life threatening.

Some have argued that access to live *Variola* virus is no longer needed for research on vaccines; however, members of the WHO advisory committee on *Variola* virus research disagreed on this in the 2004 and 2005 recommendations. Continued studies are essential to verify that newer, safer vaccines can neutralise live *Variola* virus, which is a direct indicator that antibodies are conferring virus-specific immunity. Added assurance that a replacement vaccine confers protection could come from studies with an animal model.

Currently, we have no effective antiviral drugs for smallpox infection. The basic research required to develop drugs to treat smallpox was largely discontinued when the disease was eradicated. Little work was done until 1995, when the possibility of secret stocks led US scientists to begin searching for antiviral drugs. Since then, scientists have devised assays to screen for promising compounds. But even with hundreds of laboratories at work on drug development, producing the first drug for a disease takes years, and because of the restrictions on *Variola* virus research, only the two WHO authorised laboratories can use live *Variola* virus for drug development. Nevertheless, scientists have developed three candidate drugs and have been given regulatory approval to begin evaluating their safety in humans and efficacy in primate models.

The US Food and Drug Administration requires proof that a drug is effective against live *Variola* virus before it will give it a license. This is because some drugs have shown activity against surrogates such as monkeypox virus but reduced or no activity against *Variola* virus. The process to complete the necessary studies to convince national drug regulatory agencies that such drugs are safe and effective can be lengthy.

Better Diagnostic Tests

Since health care professionals have not seen cases of smallpox for almost 30 years, it is likely early cases would be misdiagnosed or undiagnosed. In the event of an outbreak, public health officials will need better laboratory diagnostic abilities to enable early, accurate recognition and response efforts. In the report of its seventh meeting, the WHO advisory committee notes that reference laboratories might need more than one diagnostic test reliably to distinguish *Variola* virus infection from infection with other orthopoxviruses. Accurate diagnosis is especially important given the serious consequences of misdiagnosing smallpox. Although various laboratories have developed several new diagnostic tests, they require validation.

The development and licensure of better diagnostics, safe and effective drugs, and safer vaccines against smallpox will take time. Setting an arbitrary date to complete scientific research is premature and short sighted. As long as there is a possibility that terrorists could use smallpox to wreak havoc, WHO-supervised research must continue so scientists can develop the tools needed to combat an outbreak of smallpox effectively and efficiently.

"In order to avoid an international confrontation over smallpox virus destruction . . . Washington should be prepared
to negotiate a compromise formula that
breaks the current deadlock."

The United States Should Negotiate a Compromise Regarding the Retention of the Smallpox Virus

Jonathan B. Tucker

Jonathan B. Tucker suggests in the following viewpoint that the United States propose a compromise with regard to the debate about destroying the smallpox virus. Tucker suggests specific is-sues be included in the compromise such as the destruction of most of the retained virus stocks, the establishment of roles and penalties regarding the possession and research of the virus, and the provision of antiviral drugs to other countries. Tucker is a chemical and biological weapons expert and has written several articles and books, including Toxic Terror: Assessing Terrorist Use of Chemical and Biological Weapons.

Jonathan B. Tucker, "The Smallpox Destruction Debate: Could a Grand Bargain Settle the Issue?" *Arms Control Today*, March 2009, pp. 6–7, 9, 12–15. Copyright © 2009 Arms Control Association. Reproduced by permission.

As you read, consider the following questions:

1. Why did the World Health Organization (WHO) in 1999 approve a research program to develop medical countermeasures against smallpox, according to the author?

2. Does Jonathan B. Tucker propose that the destruction of selected smallpox virus stocks occur all at once or in stages?

3. In the author's opinion, why is it important for the United States to assist other countries in establishing national disease surveillance and reporting systems?

One of the longest and most contentious international policy debates has swirled around the question of whether to destroy the last known stocks of the smallpox (variola) virus, which are preserved at two World Health Organization (WHO) authorized repositories in Russia and the United States. Although smallpox was eradicated from nature more than three decades ago, concerns surfaced in the early 1990s that a few countries may have retained undeclared samples of the virus for biological warfare purposes. Because a smallpox outbreak would be a global public health emergency of major proportions, in 1999 the WHO approved a research program at the two authorized repositories to develop improved medical defenses against the disease. . . .

Charting the Smallpox Virus

A contagious viral disease that infected only humans and had a mortality rate of about 30 percent, smallpox claimed hundreds of millions of lives over the course of history and left the survivors with disfiguring facial scars. In 1966 the WHO launched a global vaccination campaign that over the next 11 years eradicated smallpox from the planet in one of the greatest public health achievements of the 20th century. . . .

In 1983 two facilities, the U.S. Center for Disease Control [and Prevention] (CDC) in Atlanta and the State Research Institute for Viral Preparations in Moscow, became the sole authorized repositories of the smallpox virus. These two sites were chosen because they had served as the WHO reference laboratories during the eradication campaign and thus possessed the world's largest collections of smallpox virus strains. But the poor physical security at the Moscow institute, combined with the political unrest that followed the breakup of the Soviet Union, prompted fears that the smallpox virus stocks stored there might be at risk. In 1994, without obtaining prior approval from the WHO, the Russian government moved the repository from Moscow to the State Research Center of Virology and Biotechnology "Vector" in the remote Siberian town of Koltsovo, near Novosibirsk. Today the CDC has 451 samples of 229 different strains of the smallpox virus, collected from outbreaks in various parts of the world during the eradication campaign, while Vector has 691 samples of 120 strains. At each repository, the virus stocks are stored in liquid-nitrogen freezers and protected with elaborate security measures.

In 1990 a WHO scientific advisory committee recommended that all known stocks of the smallpox virus be destroyed by December 31, 1993, after the DNA sequences of representative strains had been determined for scientific and forensic purposes. Protests from the scientific community and delays in the DNA sequencing effort led the WHO to postpone the date of destruction. Meanwhile, in 1992 a high-level official in the Soviet biological warfare program named Kanatjan Alibekov (aka Ken Alibek) defected to the United States with some stunning information. He told the CIA [Central Intelligence Agency] that during the Cold War, the Soviet Union had developed a highly lethal strain of the smallpox virus as a strategic weapon and had produced and stockpiled several tons of the virus in the form of a liquid suspension.

Particularly troubling was Alibek's claim that the Vector laboratory had been directly involved in the weaponization of smallpox. Moreover, the secret development and production program had been in systematic noncompliance with the 1972 Biological Weapons Convention (BWC), to which Moscow was a party.

The Threats of Existing Smallpox Stores

Alibek's revelations suggested that Russia and other states might have retained hidden caches of the smallpox virus in violation of WHO policy. The CIA subsequently obtained circumstantial evidence that undeclared stocks of the virus might exist in several countries of proliferation concern, possibly including but not necessarily limited to Iran, Iraq, and North Korea. A few scientific research centers also reported finding and destroying vials containing the smallpox virus that had been retained inadvertently in laboratory freezers, sparking fears that other poorly secured samples might exist that could fall into the hands of terrorists.

These preoccupations, combined with the progressive decline in the proportion of the global population with persistent immunity to smallpox, the limited supplies of the smallpox vaccine, the lack of physician familiarity with the disease, and the increased density and mobility of urban dwellers in megacities throughout the developing world, stoked fears that a deliberate release of smallpox virus by a rogue state or terrorist group could result in a rapidly spreading epidemic, posing a grave threat to international health and security. Most Americans born after 1972, except those who had served in the armed forces or traveled to countries where the disease was endemic, had not been immunized against smallpox and hence would be unprotected during an outbreak, while those vaccinated once in childhood were believed to retain only partial immunity. The vulnerability to smallpox of much of the world's population could not be remedied by a return to universal vaccination because the standard vaccine was not risk free. Although the adverse effects, including the rare death, associated with the vaccination of otherwise healthy people could be tolerated when natural smallpox was widespread, these risks became unacceptable once the disease was eradicated. Moreover, no antiviral drugs had been licensed for the treatment of smallpox.

In 1996 the World Health Assembly adopted Resolution 49.10 recommending that the smallpox virus stocks at the CDC and Vector be destroyed on June 30, 1999. Over the next few years, however, the United States became increasingly concerned about the possible existence of undeclared stocks of the virus and the lack of effective medical defenses. In 1998 the U.S. government asked the Institute of Medicine, a policy analysis arm of the National Academy of Sciences, to assess the scientific need for additional research with the smallpox virus. An Institute of Medicine expert committee released a report in March 1999 endorsing further work with the live virus to develop improved diagnostic tools, a safer vaccine, and at least two antiviral drugs that worked by different mechanisms. The rationale was that in the event of a bioterrorist attack with the smallpox virus, the contagion might spread widely before large-scale vaccination could begin. Thus, therapeutic drugs would be needed to treat the first generation of cases and to help contain the epidemic.

Responding to U.S. pressure, the World Health Assembly in May 1999 adopted Resolution 52.10 establishing a three-year program of applied research with the smallpox virus at the two authorized repositories. . . .

Although the United States wanted the smallpox research program to be open-ended, India insisted on amending the resolution to state that all work with the live virus would cease at the end of 2002 unless the World Health Assembly made a positive decision to extend it. The draft resolution, as amended, was adopted by acclamation. In May 2002, following the fall 2001 terrorist attacks and anthrax mailings in the United States, the World Health Assembly adopted Resolution 55.15, which extended the smallpox research program at the CDC and Vector for an indefinite period and put off a decision on the timing of virus destruction until all of the research goals had been achieved. . . .

Averting a Diplomatic Disaster

Now that the WHO-approved smallpox research program has reached the 10-year mark and many of its primary objectives have been accomplished, the international debate over virus destruction has re-emerged with a new intensity. Because the developing countries of Africa and Asia suffered disproportionately from the ravages of smallpox during the decades prior to eradication, they have a strong emotional stake in the issue and view the continued existence of the virus as a potential threat. At the 2006 World Health Assembly, 46 states from WHO's Africa region, supported by Jordan, Iran, and Thailand, tabled a draft resolution setting a new deadline of June 30, 2010, for destroying the smallpox virus stocks at the CDC and Vector. The United States, Russia, and a few other countries blocked adoption of the resolution. . . .

In order to avoid an international confrontation over smallpox virus destruction that would be harmful to all concerned, Washington should be prepared to negotiate a compromise formula that breaks the current deadlock. Such a grand bargain might consist of the following elements.

Reduce the Smallpox Virus Stocks. Russia and the United States would agree to reduce the WHO-authorized stocks of the smallpox virus at the CDC and Vector to a small number of representative strains, perhaps 10 at each repository, and to halt all research with the live virus after two effective antiviral drugs have been developed and licensed. Skeptics might argue that destroying most but not all of the virus stocks is like being "a little bit pregnant" and would not satisfy hard-line de-

Who Is WHO?

WHO [the World Health Organization] is the directing and coordinating authority for health within the United Nations system. It is responsible for providing leadership on global health matters, shaping the health research agenda, setting norms and standards, articulating evidence-based policy options, providing technical support to countries and monitoring and assessing health trends.

WHO fulfils its objectives through its core functions:

- providing leadership on matters critical to health and engaging in partnerships where joint action is needed;

- shaping the research agenda and stimulating the generation translation and dissemination of valuable knowledge;

- setting norms and standards and promoting and monitoring their implementation;

- articulating ethical and evidence-based policy options;

- providing technical support, catalysing change, and building sustainable institutional capacity; and

- monitoring the health situation and assessing health trends.

The World Health Organization,
"About WHO," 2009. www.who.int.

structionists. Nevertheless, because Moscow and Washington so far have been entirely unresponsive to the concerns of other countries, the admittedly symbolic action of destroying most of the virus stocks under their control would be a major step toward reconciliation. Destruction would occur in stages, beginning with the strains that are least valuable scientifically, such as the 14 hybrids of the smallpox virus and animal pox-viruses (rabbitpox and cowpox) that were prepared by British virologist Keith Dumbell and transferred to the CDC collection. The Advisory Committee on Variola Virus Research found no scientific rationale for further study of the hybrid strains and has recommended repeatedly that they be destroyed. Next on the list for elimination would be roughly 200 strains held at the CDC for which no epidemiological information is available about the clinical effects of the virus in humans. The small number of strains to be retained indefinitely at each repository would be stored under the highest levels of physical security in case there is a scientific need for them in the future. Because most but not all of the virus stocks in Russia and the United States would be eliminated, the standard of evidence required for verification would be less demanding and hence politically more feasible than for complete destruction.

Reaffirm Existing Rules and Impose Criminal Penalties. All WHO member states would formally acknowledge the threat posed by the potential de novo [a new] synthesis of the small-pox virus and reaffirm the existing rules that (a) strictly forbid the chemical synthesis of full-length smallpox virus genomes or their assembly from smaller DNA fragments, (b) prohibit any laboratory outside the two WHO-authorized repositories from holding DNA that comprises more than 20 percent of the smallpox virus genome, (c) ban any genetic engineering of the smallpox virus or the insertion of smallpox viral genes into other poxviruses, (d) require all laboratories outside the two authorized repositories to obtain permission from the WHO to synthesize fragments of smallpox virus DNA longer than 500 base pairs, and (e) authorize the distribution of short fragments of smallpox viral DNA to outside labs that request them through the WHO but permit transfers to third parties only with WHO approval. Under the grand bargain, all member states would pledge to adopt national legislation imposing severe criminal penalties on anyone who breaks these rules and encouraging scientists to report violations to the appropriate national authorities. To facilitate reporting without risk of retaliation, anonymous hotlines or Web sites might be set up for this purpose.

Provide Assistance. To demonstrate the value of smallpox research for the developing world, Russia and the United States would provide assurances that intellectual property rights to drugs or vaccines developed by the research program will be made available free of charge to countries that wish to manufacture them. In addition, Moscow and Washington would contribute to a fund to establish a WHO-controlled stockpile of antiviral drugs for rapid deployment to treat the victims of a smallpox attack, and would increase their allocation of smallpox vaccine to the Global Smallpox Vaccine Reserve maintained by the WHO. Finally, given that smallpox can spread readily from person to person, it is in the interest of all countries to contain an outbreak close to the source, wherever it occurs. To improve the international capacity for prompt detection and containment of smallpox and other epidemic diseases, the United States would offer developing countries technical and financial assistance in setting up national disease surveillance and reporting systems, including diagnostic laboratories, thereby helping them to fulfill the requirements of the revised International Health Regulations.

Make Antiviral Drugs Available to African Countries. The United States would make medical countermeasures developed under the smallpox research program available for combating monkeypox, a human disease that closely resembles smallpox but is considerably less lethal and transmissible. Monkeypox is endemic in the Democratic Republic of Congo (DRC) and, in a less virulent form, the rainforest countries of West Africa. Unlike smallpox, it infects rodents and monkeys as well as humans. (In the summer of 2003, a shipment of infected rodents from Ghana destined for the exotic pet trade caused an outbreak of monkeypox in the United States.) Ever since routine vaccination against smallpox ended, the incidence of monkeypox in Africa has risen in parallel with the proportion of the population that is unvaccinated, and the disease now has the potential to establish itself in humans through person-to-person transmission. Unfortunately, mass vaccination against monkeypox in the DRC may not be possible because of the increasing prevalence of HIV/AIDS infection, which suppresses the immune system and renders the smallpox vaccine less effective and potentially life threatening. However, the antiviral drugs developed to treat smallpox should be effective against monkeypox as well. Once these drugs have been licensed, the United States would agree to make them available at a subsidized price or free of charge for the purpose of treating monkeypox in the affected African countries.

Inspect Smallpox Repositories for Security Purposes. The World Health Assembly would request the WHO secretariat to continue making periodic inspections of the smallpox virus repositories in Russia and the United States to ensure that the residual stocks continue to be stored in a safe and highly secure manner.

Such a grand bargain, or a similar negotiating formula, would aim to bridge the gap between the pro-destruction and anti-destruction camps. The proposed foreign assistance programs would generate goodwill throughout the developing world and might be seen as a reasonable quid pro quo for the continued retention of a small number of smallpox viral strains at the two authorized repositories as a hedge against future developments. In any event, creative diplomacy will be needed to break out of the current deadlock and bring the protracted and contentious debate over smallpox virus destruction to a broadly acceptable conclusion.

Periodical Bibliography

The following articles have been selected to supplement the diverse views presented in this chapter.

Arms Control
Association

"Reducing Biological Risks to Security: International Policy Recommendations for the Obama Administration," January 2009. http://armscontrol.org.

Mark D'Agostino
and Greg Martin

"The Bioscience Revolution and the Biological Weapons Threat: Levers and Interventions," *Globalization and Health*, February 2009.

Malcolm Dando

"Bioethicists Enter the Dual-Use Debate," *Bulletin of the Atomic Scientists*, April 20, 2009.

Gigi Kwik Gronvall,
et al.

"Priorities for Preventing a Biological Attack That Should Emerge from the WMD Commission Report," Center for Biosecurity, January 22, 2009.

Stephen M. Maurer

"Grassroot Efforts to Impede Bioterrorism," *Bulletin of the Atomic Scientists*, March 5, 2009.

Robin McDowell

"U.S. Controls Bird Flu Vaccines over Bioweapon Fears," Associated Press, October 11, 2008.

MSNBC

"Destruction of Smallpox Virus Delayed Again," May 18, 2007. www.msnbc.com.

National
Intelligence Council

"Global Trends 2025: A Transformed World," November 2008.

Judy Winters

"The National Bio Agro Defense Facility's 'Dual Use' Research, a Threat to Our Nation's Security," *OpEd News*, April 29, 2008. www.opednews.com.

For Further Discussion

Chapter 1

1. Allison Macfarlane believes that biological weapons should not be included in the same category as nuclear weapons nor given equal defense funding. In your opinion, do biological weapons pose a threat greater than, lesser than, or equal to the threat of nuclear weapons? Explain your answer.

2. According to Jeffrey W. Runge, the risk of an anthrax attack is significant and the result could be catastrophic; however, Fred Burton and Scott Stewart maintain that the risk has been considerably overblown. Whose argument do you believe is more convincing and why?

3. Stefan Riedel writes about the ever-present danger of a smallpox epidemic because stocks of the virus still exist. Do you believe Americans should be vaccinated against smallpox? Why or why not?

Chapter 2

1. According to Robert S. Mueller III, foreign and domestic terrorist groups are determined to attack the United States with biological weapons in the near future. Milton Leitenberg, however, maintains that the imminence of biological warfare has been deliberately exaggerated. Whose evidence do you find more compelling? Explain your answer.

2. James Thuo Njuguna explains that outbreaks of many infectious diseases known to be potential biological weapons are prevalent in regions of Africa. Do you believe that infectious disease outbreaks in Africa can undermine the security of the United States? Explain.

Chapter 3

1. Many Americans believe that biodefense research laboratories are necessary for the protection of the United States against infectious disease threats. After reading the viewpoints of Edward Hammond and Hugh Auchincloss, do you agree or disagree? Are there any safety risks to the public that concern you? Defend your answer with evidence from the viewpoints.

2. Richard Burr maintains that research involving select agents needs increased oversight, while Gigi Kwik Gronvall worries that too many restrictions could disrupt important research collaboration. Where do you think the balance between research and public safety should be? Explain your answer.

3. After reading the viewpoint of Tara O'Toole, do you feel the United States government is prepared for a biological warfare attack? Do you know if your city has a disaster preparedness plan? In your opinion, is such a plan important?

Chapter 4

1. Jeanne Guillemin and John C. Rood maintain that the Biological Weapons Convention is significant in the prevention of biological warfare. In your opinion, should national interests be a higher priority than global security? Explain your answer.

2. Although smallpox was eradicated in 1977, stocks of the virus were retained for future research. Edward Hammond maintains that all stocks of the smallpox virus should be destroyed, John O. Agwunobi insists that destroying the virus stocks would be ill-advised, and Jonathan B. Tucker suggests a compromise is in order. Whose argument do you find most compelling? Use the viewpoints to find specific reasons for your answer.

Organizations to Contact

The editors have compiled the following list of organizations concerned with the issues debated in this book. The descriptions are derived from materials provided by the organizations. All have publications or information available for interested readers. The list was compiled on the date of publication of the present volume; the information provided here may change. Be aware that many organizations take several weeks or longer to respond to inquiries, so allow as much time as possible.

Arms Control Association (ACA)
1313 L Street NW, Suite 130, Washington, DC   20005
(202) 463-8270 • fax: (202) 463-8273
e-mail: aca@armscontrol.org
Web site: www.armscontrol.org

The Arms Control Association (ACA) is a national membership organization that works to educate the public and promote effective arms control policies. It publishes the magazine *Arms Control Today*. Documents, fact sheets, briefs, and reports on biological weapons and the Biological and Toxin Weapons Convention (BTWC) can be found on its Web site.

Brookings Institution
1775 Massachusetts Avenue NW, Washington, DC   20036
(202) 797-6000 • fax: (202) 797-6004
e-mail: communications@brookings.edu
Web site: www.brookings.edu

The Brookings Institution, founded in 1927, is a nonprofit public policy organization that conducts research and education in foreign policy, economics, government, and the social sciences. Its publications include the periodic *Policy Briefs*, weekly newsletter *Metro Update*, and weekly e-mail report *Brookings Alert*.

Center for Biosecurity of University of Pittsburgh Medical Center

The Pier IV Building, 621 East Pratt Street, Suite 210
Baltimore, MD   21202
(443) 573-3304 • fax: (443) 573-3305

The Center for Biosecurity is an independent, nonprofit organization of the University of Pittsburgh Medical Center (UPMC) that seeks to strengthen national security by reducing the risks posed by biological attacks, epidemics, and other destabilizing events, and to improve the nation's resilience in the face of such events. The center publishes the journal *Biosecurity and Bioterrorism* and the daily *Biosecurity News in Brief*, which provides links to current information and articles.

Center for Infectious Disease Research & Policy (CIDRAP)

University of Minnesota, Academic Health Center
420 Delaware Street SE, MMC 263, Minneapolis, MN   55455
(612) 626-6770 • fax: (612) 626-6783
e-mail: cidrap@umn.edu
Web site: www.cidrap.umn.edu

Center for Infectious Disease Research & Policy (CIDRAP)is a member of the Consortium on Law and Values in Health, Environment & the Life Sciences, which supports work on the legal, ethical, and policy implications of problems in health, environment, and the life sciences. Its goal is to advance knowledge, public understanding, and sound policy. The center publishes weekly e-mail briefings called *CIDRAP Business Source*, with a specific section of links to published articles about bioterrorism.

Center for Strategic & International Studies (CSIS)

1800 K Street NW, Washington, DC   20006
(202) 887-0200 • fax: (202) 775-3199
Web site: www.csis.org

The Center for Strategic & International Studies (CSIS) works to provide world leaders with strategic insights and policy options on current and emerging global issues. It publishes *The*

Challenge of Biological Terrorism, reports, newsletters, commentaries, and *Critical Questions*, which focuses on international public policy issues.

Centers for Disease Control and Prevention (CDC)

1600 Clifton Road, Atlanta, GA   30333
(800) 232-4636
e-mail: cdcinfo@cdc.gov
Web site: www.cdc.gov

The Centers for Disease Control and Prevention (CDC) is the government agency charged with protecting the public health of the nation by preventing and controlling diseases and by responding to public health emergencies. The center publishes the journals *Emerging Infectious Diseases*, *Preventing Chronic Disease*, and *Morbidity and Mortality Weekly Report*. Information on potential biological warfare agents including anthrax and smallpox is available on the CDC's Web site.

Federation of American Scientists (FAS)

1725 DeSales Street NW, 6th Floor, Washington, DC   20036
(202) 546-3300 • fax: (202) 675-1010
e-mail: fas@fas.org
Web site: www.fas.org

The Federation of American Scientists (FAS) is a privately funded, nonprofit organization engaged in analysis and advocacy on science, technology, and public policy for global security. Its Biological and Chemical Weapons Control Project concentrates on researching and advocating policies that balance science and security without compromising national security or scientific progress. That includes preventing the misuse of the federation's research and promoting public understanding of the real threats from biological and chemical weapons. The federation publishes the quarterly *FAS Public Interest Report*, articles, fact sheets, and white papers.

Food and Drug Administration (FDA)
10903 New Hampshire Avenue, Silver Spring, MD   20993
(888) 463-6332
Web site: www.fda.gov

The Food and Drug Administration (FDA) is a federal government public health agency that monitors the safety of the nation's foods and medicines. Its Web site includes a special section that focuses on emergency preparedness and response with information about possible bioterrorist attacks. Among its publications is the *Strategic Action Plan* report.

Henry L. Stimson Center
1111 Nineteenth Street NW, 12th Floor
Washington, DC   20036
(202) 223-5956 • fax: (202) 238-9604
e-mail: info@stimson.org
Web site: www.stimson.org

The Henry L. Stimson Center is an independent public policy institute committed to finding and promoting innovative solutions to the security challenges confronting the United States and other nations. The center directs the Biological and Chemical Threats Program, which focuses on "dual-use technologies." The center produces reports, papers, and books on policy regarding biological and other weapons of mass destruction, including *Old Plagues, New Threats: The Biotech Revolution and Its Impact on U.S. National Security.*

James Martin Center for Nonproliferation Studies (CMS)
Monterey Institute of International Studies, 460 Pierce Street
Monterey, CA   93940
(831) 647-4154 • fax: (831) 647-3519
e-mail: cns@miis.edu
Web site: http://cns.miis.edu

The James Martin Center for Nonproliferation Studies (CNS) is a nongovernmental organization devoted exclusively to research and training on nonproliferation issues. The CNS trains graduate students in the nonproliferation of weapons of mass destruction (WMD) and conducts seminars and provides background material for the media, educators, and the public. The center's many publications include the peer-reviewed journal *The Nonproliferation Review*. CNS also maintains databases on WMD developments and nonproliferation regimes.

Bibliography of Books

Daniel Barenblatt   *A Plague upon Humanity: The Hidden History of Japan's Biological Warfare Program.* New York: Harper Collins, 2004.

Francis Anthony Boyle   *Biowarfare and Terrorism.* Atlanta: Clarity Press, 2005.

Dan Caldwell   *Seeking Security in an Insecure World.* Lanham, MD: Rowman & Littlefield, 2005.

Michael C. Carroll   *Lab 257: The Disturbing Story of the Government's Secret Germ Laboratory.* New York: Harper Paperbacks, 2005.

Sandro K. Cinti and Philip C. Hanna   *Biological Agents of Warfare and Terrorism.* Baltimore: Lippincott, Williams & Wilkins, 2007.

William R. Clark   *Bracing for Armageddon? The Science and Politics of Bioterrorism in America.* New York: Oxford University Press, 2008.

Anne L. Clunan, Peter Lavoy, and Susan B. Martin   *Terrorism, War, or Disease?: Unraveling the Use of Biological Weapons.* Stanford, CA: Stanford University Press, 2008.

Bob Coen and Eric Nadler   *Dead Silence: Fear and Terror on the Anthrax Trail.* Berkeley, CA: Counterpoint, 2009.

Malcolm Dando   *Bioterror and Biowarfare: A Beginner's Guide.* Oxford, England: Oneworld Publications, 2006.

Jeanne Guillemin   *Biological Weapons: From the Invention of State-Sponsored Programs to Contemporary Bioterrorism.* New York: Columbia University Press, 2006.

D.A. Henderson   *Smallpox—the Death of a Disease:*
and Richard   *The Inside Story of Eradicating a*
Preston   *Worldwide Killer.* New York: Prometheus Books, 2009.

James A. Johnson   *Health Organizations: Theory, Behavior, and Development.* Sudbury, MA: Jones and Bartlett Publishers, 2009.

R. William   *Bioterror: Anthrax, Influenza, and the*
Johnstone   *Future of Public Health Security.* Santa Barbara, CA: Praeger, 2008.

Peter Katona,   *Countering Terrorism and WMD:*
John P. Sullivan,   *Creating a Global Counter-Terrorism*
and Michael   *Network.* Florence, KY: Routledge,
Intriligator   2006.

Ronald J. Kendall,   *Advances in Biological and Chemical*
et al.   *Terrorism Countermeasures.* Boca Raton, FL: CRC Press, 2008.

Jez Littlewood   *The Biological Weapons Convention: A Failed Revolution.* Hampshire, England: Ashgate Publishing, 2005.

Sue Mahan and   *Terrorism in Perspective.* Thousand
Pamela L. Griset   Oaks, CA: Sage Publications, 2008.

Gus Martin   *Understanding Terrorism: Challenges, Perspectives, and Issues.* Thousand Oaks, CA: Sage Publications, 2009.

Thomas R. Mockaitis   *The "New" Terrorism: Myths and Reality.* Stanford, CA: Stanford University Press, 2008.

Fathali M. Moghaddam   *From the Terrorists' Point of View: What They Experience and Why They Come to Destroy.* Santa Barbara, CA: Praeger Security International, 2006.

Marion Nestle   *Safe Food: Bacteria, Biotechnology, and Bioterrorism.* Berkeley, CA: University of California Press, 2003.

John Parachini   *Motives, Means and Mayhem: Terrorist Acquisition and Use of Unconventional Weapons.* Washington, DC: Rand Corporation, 2005.

Richard Preston   *Panic in Level 4: Cannibals, Killer Viruses, and Other Journeys to the Edge of Science.* New York: Random House, 2009.

Richard Preston   *The Demon in the Freezer.* New York: Fawcett Books, 2003.

Sergey N. Rumyantsev   *Biological Weapon: A Terrible Reality? Profound Delusion? Skillful Swindling?* New York: Vantage Press, 2006.

Jeffrey R. Ryan and Jan F. Glarum   *Biosecurity and Bioterrorism: Containing and Preventing Biological Threats.* Burlington, MA: Elsevier, 2008.

Jonathan B. Tucker — *Scourge: The Once and Future Threat of Smallpox.* New York: Atlantic Monthly Press, 2001.

Geoffrey L. Zubay, et al. — *Agents of Bioterrorism: Pathogens and Their Weaponization.* New York: Columbia University Press, 2005.

Index